ABOUT THE AUTHOR

Dr. Anna Lydia Motto is Professor of Classics at the University of South Florida in Tampa. She received her B.A. degree from Queens College, an M.A. from New York University, and the Ph.D. in 1953 from the University of North Carolina, where she held a Fellowship. She has received a number of research awards, as well as a Fulbright Grant to the American Academy in Rome.

Dr. Motto is a recognized authority and distinguished scholar in the field of Senecan studies. Her publications include the book-length study, *Seneca Sourcebook: Guide to the Thought of Lucius Annaeus Seneca* (Amsterdam: Adolf Hakkert, 1970), together with more than fifteen scholarly articles on this philosopher. In addition, she has co-edited with her husband, Dr. John R. Clark, *Satire: An Anthology* (New York: G. P. Putnam's Sons, 1972), and has published articles on Homer, Theocritus, Catullus, Horace, and Juvenal. She has also delivered many papers before various Classical societies. Her studies and reviews have appeared in the *American Journal of Philology, Arethusa, Classical Bulletin, Classical Journal, Classical Outlook, Classical Philology, Classical World, Satire Newsletter,* and the *Transactions of the American Philological Association.*

Previously, Dr. Motto has taught at Washington College, Muhlenberg College, Alfred University, Drew University, the University of North Carolina, and St. John's University. In 1969 she served as Visiting Professor of Classics at the University of Michigan in Ann Arbor. Currently, Dr. Motto is Vice President of The Classical Association of the Atlantic States.

TWAYNE'S WORLD AUTHORS SERIES

A Survey of the World's Literature

Sylvia E. Bowman, Indiana University

GENERAL EDITOR

LATIN LITERATURE

Philip Levine, University of California

EDITOR

Seneca

(TWAS 268)

TWAYNE'S WORLD AUTHORS SERIES (TWAS)

*The purpose of TWAS is to survey the major writers
—novelists, dramatists, historians, poets, philoso-
phers, and critics—of the nations of the world.
Among the national literatures covered are those of
Australia, Canada, China, Eastern Europe, France,
Germany, Greece, India, Italy, Japan, Latin America,
the Netherlands, New Zealand, Poland, Russia, Scan-
dinavia, Spain, and the African nations, as well as
Hebrew, Yiddish, and Latin Classical literatures.
This survey is complemented by Twayne's United
States Authors Series and English Authors Series.*

*The intent of each volume in these series is to present
a critical analytical study of the works of the writer;
to include biographical and historical material that
may be necessary for understanding, appreciation,
and critical appraisal of the writer; and to present all
material in clear, concise English—but not to vitiate
the scholarly content of the work by doing so.*

Seneca

By ANNA LYDIA MOTTO

University of South Florida

Twayne Publishers, Inc.　：：　New York

For Jack

Consortium rerum omnium inter nos facit amicitia

Preface

SENECA

I wish to thank the Editors of the *American Journal of Philology, Classical Bulletin, Classical Journal, Classical Outlook,* and *Classical Philology,* for permitting me to include material in this book which appeared in somewhat different form in their journals.

Sincerest acknowledgment is extended to Professors Sylvia Bowman and Philip Levine for having given me the opportunity to write this book. Moreover, I wish to express special and deepest gratitude to my husband, Dr. John R. Clark, who has often collaborated with me and constantly encouraged me in my Senecan studies.

ANNA LYDIA MOTTO

Contents

Chronology

(All dates are A.D., except where otherwise indicated.)

31 B.C.–
A.D. 14 Reign of Augustus
C. 4 B.C. Seneca born at Cordova, Spain. Brought to Rome when a very young child. Receives grammatical, rhetorical, and philosophical training.

14–37 Reign of Tiberius
Visits Egypt in his early twenties. Returns to Rome, 31. Begins active public career, becoming quaestor about 33, and perhaps aedile or tribune of the plebs about 36 or 37.

37–41 Reign of Caligula
Enjoys reputation as renowned orator and highly popular writer. His ability and eloquence arouse the jealousy of the mad Caligula. Abandons his perilous oratorical career. Death of his father about 39.

41–54 Reign of Claudius
Holds socially prominent position in the court of Claudius. Unjustly accused by Messalina, the emperor's third wife, of illicit relations with the Princess Julia, and exiled from Rome to Corsica. Spends eight years of his life (41–49) in remote, barbaric Corsica. Recalled in 49 by Agrippina, Claudius' fourth wife, to become tutor to Nero, her young son. Agrippina obtains for him the praetorship and places him in the senate.

54–68 Reign of Nero
For five years, from the accession of the seventeen-year-old Nero in 54 until 59—a period known as the Quin-

quennium Neronis—Seneca, with the aid of Burrus, prefect of the guard, curbs Nero's excesses and administers
affairs in Rome with equity and kindness. Death of
Burrus in 62; Seneca requests permission from Nero to
retire but is refused. Though not officially released from
court, Seneca commences a life of self-exile, seclusion,
and study. These years of retirement, 62–65, constitute
the *anni mirabiles* of Seneca's literary career. After the
great fire in Rome, 64, Seneca again attempts to retire at
a considerable distance from the court and city, but Nero
again refuses. Seneca accused of complicity in the Pisonian Conspiracy, 65, which had as its object the murder of
Nero. Suicide-death of Seneca in 65, by order of the
emperor.

Chronology of the Senecan Corpus

A LTHOUGH scholars have long toiled to establish a precise chronology for Seneca's works, the problem of dating remains unresolved.[1] In the following table, I have listed, after each of the extant works, what appears to be a likely date.

EXTANT WORKS:

Dialogi[2]:
    De Providentia (Dial. I) c. A.D. 63–64
    De Constantia Sapientis (Dial. II) c. 54–56
    De Ira libri tres (Dial. III, IV, V) Bks. I–II, c. 41; Bk. III, c. 49
    Ad Marciam de Consolatione (Dial. VI) c. 40–41
    De Vita Beata (Dial. VII) c. 58–59
    De Otio (Dial. VIII) c. 62
    De Tranquillitate Animi (Dial. IX) c. 59–61
    De Brevitate Vitae (Dial. X) c. 49
    Ad Polybium de Consolatione (Dial. XI) c. 43–44
    Ad Helviam Matrem de Consolatione (Dial. XII) c. 41–42
De Clementia c. 55–56
De Beneficiis c. 58–63
Quaestiones Naturales c. 62–64
Epistulae Morales ad Lucilium c. 62–65
Apocolocyntosis (Ludus de Morte Claudii) c. 54
Tragoediae[3]: c. 45–55
    Hercules Furens
    Troades
    Phoenissae
    Medea
    Phaedra
    Oedipus

Agamemnon
Thyestes
Hercules Oetaeus
Octavia (?)
Epigrammata super exilio[4] c. 41–49

LOST WORKS[5]:

De Motu Terrarum
De Lapidum Natura
De Piscium Natura
De Situ Indiae
De Situ et Sacris Aegyptiorum
De Forma Mundi
Exhortationes
De Officiis
De Immatura Morte
De Superstitione
De Matrimonio
De Amicitia
Vita Patris
Orationes[6]
Epistulae ad Novatum
Moralis Philosophiae Libri
De Remediis Fortuitorum

CHAPTER 1

Seneca's Life

A MONG the outstanding personalities of imperial Rome there is no one who can more readily arouse our interest and admiration than Lucius Annaeus Seneca. Tutor, guardian, minister, victim of Nero, author of tragedies, scientific treatises, philosophical essays, and moral epistles, he was a man to honor—and to serve—any age. Living in an era of universal tyranny and corruption, he was forced to share his destiny with Nero, *parricida matris et uxoris, auriga et histrio et incendiarius* ("murderer of mother and wife, jockey, actor, and arsonist").[1] Consigned to such a precipice of history, it is the more amazing that this rich courtier and polished orator not only transmitted Stoic philosophy to the world, but altered and enhanced it, its doctrines becoming in his hands something warm, sprightly, personal, humane. In a cold and desperate century, his prose is full of feeling, eloquence, and profound thought. And his influence has been enduring: in the Renaissance alone, one must turn repeatedly back to Seneca to understand the origins of the essay, the compelling tragedies of the Elizabethan theater, the nature of seventeenth-century style itself. His extant writings constitute a staunch body of wit and wisdom that have justly earned for him a significant place in the annals of civilization.

I Childhood and Education

Born at Cordova, in Spain about 4 B.C., Seneca came from a family of wealth and culture. His father, Seneca the Elder, was the well-known rhetor who, in his old age, transcribed from memory, at the request of his three sons, his recollections of the most renowned rhetoricians of his time. In the so-called *Controversiae* and *Suasoriae,* the elder Seneca presented themes argued in the schools of rhetoric. His work, containing many interesting digressions, anecdotes, criticisms, and quotations, is significant for the glimpses it reveals of Roman oratory in the early empire.

This distinguished father, referred to by Seneca the Younger as *virorum optimus, pater meus* ("my father, best of men," *Ad Helv.* 17.4), undoubtedly exercised a profound influence upon his sons. Equestrian in rank, old-fashioned and strict (*Ad Helv.* 17.3), he was eager to have his sons obtain prominent posts in Roman politics.

No less attractive and interesting a personality was Seneca's mother, Helvia. Younger than her husband by about thirty years, she was a woman of unusual character, ability, and intellect. In the *Ad Helviam,* the philosopher son pays highest tribute to his devoted mother. Well trained in a household that was rigorously disciplined and traditional, she lacked all of woman's normal weaknesses (*Ad Helv.* 16.2–5) and knew how bravely to overcome misfortunes that befell her (*Ad Helv.* 2.4–5). She had, moreover, a deep interest in philosophy and the liberal arts and would have pursued these studies to a fuller degree, had her husband, a rigid follower of ancestral customs, not opposed higher learning for women (*Ad Helv.* 17.4). In addition to a philosophic bent, Helvia possessed *joie d'esprit* and the ability to bestow happiness on others (*Ad Helv.* 15.1–2). Such was her devotion to her family, such her unselfishness and generosity that Seneca writes: "In your children's good fortune you ever delighted, never abusing it; you always restrained our generosity, but never your own" (*Ad Helv.* 14.3).

Seneca the Elder and Helvia had three sons—all of whom achieved some distinction. Novatus, the oldest, pursued a political career, attaining the rank of consul. To him, an accomplished orator and writer, Seneca dedicated his Dialogues *On Anger* and *On the Happy Life.* He was adopted by the rhetor, L. Junius Gallio, a friend of Seneca the Elder, and known thereafter as "Gallio." He is especially remembered for having had St. Paul come before his tribunal when he was proconsul of Achaea in 51–52.[2]

The youngest son, Mela, who pursued a career of money-making rather than one of scholarly activities or political glory, enjoys a passport to fame not through any special merit of his own but because he was the father of the poet Lucan.

By far the most renowned of these three sons was Lucius Annaeus Seneca. When a very young child, Seneca left Spain for Rome, where his entire family established permanent residence. On this journey he was carried in the arms of his maternal aunt who later became wife of the governor of Egypt. Similar in nature to his mother Helvia, this affectionate aunt was regarded by her nephew as a woman of wisdom and perfection. She it was who nursed him through illness and later on aided him when he sought the quaestorship (*Ad Helv.* 19.2–6).

Although from childhood on Seneca was of delicate health,[3] he learned to endure his physical condition by the disciplined pursuit of mental activity. Regarding one of his serious ailments, he writes: "I shall tell you what then consoled me, stating first of all that the very meditations in which I found comfort had the effect of medicine. Honorable consolations lead to a cure, and whatever has elevated the soul helps the body also. My studies were my salvation. I owe it to philosophy that I rose from my bed and regained my strength. I owe my life to philosophy" (*Ep.* 78.3).

Prior to philosophic training, the young Seneca received instruction from a *grammaticus*. Similar to present-day linguists and grammarians, the *grammaticus* could offer broad training in language and literature, even in the humanities themselves, or he could be an unimaginative, narrow pedant, an idolater of particles and *minutiae*. Unfortunately, Seneca's teacher appears to have been of the latter stamp, and in his maturity Seneca recollected his education at the hands of the grammarian as trifling. "The *grammaticus* dotes upon language . . . the enunciation of syllables, the fondling of words, the memorization of theatrical pieces, the cultivation of laws of versification—which of these abolishes fear, outlaws desire, or bridles lust?" (*Ep.* 88.3)[4]

If bored by the teachings of the *grammaticus*, Seneca was captivated by the training he received from renowned masters of rhetoric—Mamercus Scaurus, Junius Gallio, Musa, Julius Bassus.[5] Seneca the Elder, who carefully supervised the education of his sons, paid special attention that considerable emphasis be placed upon rhetoric and was, in reality, Seneca's earliest teacher of this art. According to his diligent father, oratorical training not only served to sharpen the mind but was also a significant tool for advancement in the *cursus honorum*. Guided by a father who was himself an outstanding rhetor and intimate friend of leading rhetoricians, the youthful Seneca was imbued with a decisive appreciation for eloquence and able discourse. In later years his brilliant style vividly attests to this early environment.

Yet rhetoric was not Seneca's major interest. His true love was reserved for philosophy—a subject disliked by his father (*Ep.* 108.22) but encouraged by his mother. Despite his father's partiality for oratory, Seneca nonetheless comprehended fully the basic difference between rhetoric and philosophy—the former, a fascinating art of persuasion, the latter, a most ennobling art concerned with teaching man how to live well and how to perfect his soul. "Philosophy does not consist of words but of deeds. . . . She forms and fashions the soul, arranges our life, guides our actions, reveals what we should do, what we should not" (*Ep.* 16.3). "Rather different is the aim of rhetoricians who seek to win the audience's favor, rather different the aim of those who captivate the ears of young men and of idlers by their diversified and fluent method of arguing. Philosophy teaches us not to speak, but to act" (*Ep.* 20.2).

Taught by the leading philosophers of the day—Attalus, the Stoic, Sotion, the Pythagorean, Demetrius, the Cynic, Fabianus Papirius of the Sextian school, Seneca received a diverse, eclectic philosophical training. And, in reality, by combining this training with his rhetorical skill, he cultivated thought *and* action, words *and* deeds. Like the Homeric hero, he became "a speaker of words and a doer of deeds."[6] Following Stoic doctrine, he pursued both *vita contemplativa and vita activa* (*De Otio* 3.2–3; *De Tranq. An.* 17.3).

II *Political and Literary Advancement*

Seneca began his active public career toward the end of the reign of Tiberius, having attained the quaestorship about 33. Whether he held any government posts prior to that date cannot be ascertained. We cannot, in fact, with any chronological exactness, state events that took place in Seneca's life between 19 and 41. We can, however, trace the overall pattern of happenings during that period of time.

In his early twenties, his health, which had been poor since childhood, became worse. So weak and exhausted was he by illness that depression led him seriously to contemplate suicide. But he was restrained from committing this rash act by concern for his aged father. "For I reflected, not how bravely I could die, but

how he could not bravely bear the loss of me. And so I commanded myself to live" (*Ep.* 78.2).

Shortly after and perhaps because of his infirmity, in order to
have a change of climate and scene, he went to Egypt where his
maternal aunt, who had carried him in infancy to Rome, was wife
of the governor. Through this aunt's diligent and motherly care,
her nephew regained his strength (*Ad Helv.* 19.2) and culturally
profited much from his stay in Egypt. To this period one would
properly assign the lost treatise on Egyptian geography and religious customs, as well as the lost works *On Earthquakes* and
On Superstition.

We do not know the exact date of his departure from Egypt,
but we do know that he returned to Rome in 31 after having witnessed the tragic death at sea of his uncle, governor of Egypt, and
the extraordinary bravery of his aunt, who, during the shipwreck,
risked her life to rescue the corpse of her husband (*Ad Helv.*
19.4–5).

To this unusual aunt, who so energetically gave of herself to
her loved ones, Seneca owed the first significant steps in his political career. She, though by nature modest and reserved, conquered
her shyness and became ambitious for his sake, using her influence to obtain the quaestorship for him (*Ad Helv.* 19.2).

This position he held about 33, perhaps becoming aedile or
tribune of the plebs around 36 or 37. During these years of political advancement, Seneca also pursued a renowned career as a
lawyer. His terse, pointed, brilliant oratorical style, replete with
epigrammatic *sententiae,* won for him fame and immense wealth.
Moreover, his reputation as philosopher and writer likewise continued to grow. Though no work of Seneca prior to Caligula's
death (41) has come down to us, we know from Suetonius that
during Caligula's reign (37–41) Seneca was a highly popular
writer.[7] It is indeed likely that to this period belong the speeches
and poems mentioned by Quintilian[8] as well as some of the tragedies. So outstanding was Seneca's reputation as orator and writer
that his ability and eloquence aroused the jealousy of the mad
Caligula, who sneeringly described Seneca's works as "mere school
exercises" and his style as "sand without lime."[9] The emperor was,
in fact, so irate that he would have put Seneca to death had not
one of the imperial mistresses remarked that the philosopher was
about to die soon of consumption and that it was useless to kill a

man on the verge of death.[10] Many years later, Seneca, undoubt-edly referring to this incident, wrote: "Disease has postponed many a man's death and proximity to death has resulted in salva-tion" (*Ep.* 78.6; cf. 13.11).

Having almost lost his life, Seneca decided to give up his peril-ous oratorical career. Moreover, the death of his nonagenarian father, around 39, gave Seneca greater freedom to abandon ora-tory and to devote himself more and more to literature and philosophy. To this period we may assign the lost biography of his father and possibly the *Consolation of Marcia.* And it is very probable that, during this same time, Seneca gathered together material for the three books *On Anger,* which contain scathing invective against Caligula.[11]

In 41 Caligula was assassinated and his uncle Claudius was hailed emperor. Seneca—renowned statesman, orator, philosopher, author—held the spotlight in Roman society. Even Dio, for the most part hostile to Seneca, speaks of him as "a man who sur-passed in wisdom all the Romans and many others of his time."[12] Such was Seneca's enviable position. But his good fortune was soon to end.

III   *Seneca in Exile*

Holding a socially prominent position in the court of Claudius, Seneca was on intimate terms with the princesses Julia Livilla and Agrippina, Caligula's sisters,[13] daughters of Germanicus and nieces of Claudius. At the very beginning of Claudius' reign, Messalina, Claudius' third wife, unjustly accused Seneca of an illicit intrigue with Julia.[14] The empress, envious of the beautiful Julia, whom she regarded as a dangerous opponent, and suspi-cious of the rising statesman who was seen so much in the com-pany of the princess, cruelly trumped up this charge in order to protect her own political power. Even the gossiping Suetonius states that the accusation was unfounded and that no opportunity was given to Julia for defense.[15] On such a charge was Julia exiled without trial and shortly afterward put to death;[16] and by this same unproven charge, Seneca was forced to endure humiliation and disgrace. Brought to trial before a rubber-stamp Senate which was completely dominated by the whims of Messalina, he was condemned to death; but this capital punishment was, through Claudius' intervention, commuted to one of banishment.[17] So

Seneca, at the height of prosperity, was exiled to the barren, desolate isle of Corsica[18] and, as an adjunct penalty, probably suffered confiscation of half his property.[19]

For Seneca, the year 41 brought not only public misfortune but also private tragedy. Death deprived him of two of his nephews, and three weeks before he went into exile he lost his son.[20]

Burdened so heavily by domestic troubles, he was now overwhelmed by public disaster as well. One could imagine with how dejected a spirit Seneca left Rome for remote, barbaric Corsica where he was to spend eight years of his life (41–49).

Yet, in spite of such deep sorrow, Seneca endured with considerable courage the first two years of *relegatio* in Corsica. Fortified by early philosophic training and endowed with remarkable literary talent, he must have spent much time in meditation and composition during this period of forced isolation and withdrawal. Critics have expended excessive time and energy conjecturing which of Seneca's works were written during this exile, but, with the exception of the *Ad Helviam* (which all agree was written between 42 and 43) and the *Ad Polybium* (about 43), they have been unable to furnish us with any concrete evidence. Therefore, to discuss the Dialogue on *Providence* (Why, though there is a Providence, Misfortunes befall Good Men) or on *The Constancy of the Wise Man* (The Wise Man can receive neither Injury nor Insult) in biographical terms applicable to Seneca's period of exile, as for example, Waltz, Lana, and Gummere have done,[21] is of no avail. Only the *Ad Helviam* and the *Ad Polybium* can, with certainty, be cited as biographically relevant to this period.

Well versed in the genre of *Consolationes* (*Ad Helv.* 1.2) and having written, prior to his exile, the *Consolation to Marcia*, addressed to the daughter of Cremutius Cordus, on the death of her son, Seneca in the *Ad Helviam* is at his best in this mode, utilizing all his skill and ingenuity to alleviate his mother's sorrows. Employing lofty, ennobling Stoic doctrine, the philosopher argues that "the mind cannot be exiled since it is free, akin to the gods, and companionable to every world and to every age; for its thought travels throughout the sky and penetrates all past and future time" (*Ad Helv.* 11.7).

Helvia, who from childhood suffered heaviest afflictions but endured them most bravely (*Ad Helv.* 2.1–4), must not now grieve for her son who prepared himself to meet Fortune's blows by al-

ways regarding her gifts—money, honor, influence—as fleeting,
unstable, perishable possessions that can give man no lasting joy
(*Ad Helv.* 5.1–5). True happiness, he urges, depends upon a mind
that utilizes but is not enslaved by fickle Fortune's gifts. For such
a mind, exile is but a change of place (*Ad Helv.* 6.1). Wherever
the banished man goes, he will take with him the universal beauty
of nature and his own virtue (*Ad Helv.* 8.2). So one can be, as
Seneca tries to convince his mother that he is, happy in any place,
under any conditions (*Ad Helv.* 4.1–3; 20.1–2). Helvia, therefore,
must not grieve for him nor for herself. With genuine warmth, he
exhorts her to find consolation for his absence in the remaining
beloved members of her family—her two others sons, her grand-
son Marcus, her granddaughter Novatilla, her father, her wise
and courageous sister (*Ad Helv.* 18–19).

Thus did Seneca endeavor to console his mother and indeed to
console himself—for obviously Seneca suffered, as any man would
in exile, the torments of tedium and despair. To be sure, meditation, study, and composition helped alleviate his loneliness but
were not sufficient to eradicate his extreme ennui, his burning
desire to be with his family and friends, his intense yearning to
return to Roman society. In fact, he became so despondent that,
shortly after, he addressed to Polybius, Claudius' erudite, influential freedman and secretary, who had recently lost his brother, a
Consolation that in thought and feeling stands in sharp contrast
to the elevated spirit displayed in the *Ad Helviam.* Now Seneca
openly admits his misery (*Ad Polyb.* 2.1; 13.3; 18.9) and resorts to
overt flattery of Polybius and the emperor Claudius in an eager
effort to obtain his recall from exile.[22]

Seneca's detractors point to this Dialogue as a basic source for
emphasizing the philosophers' inconsistencies in doctrine and his
failure to live by what he preached. These hostile critics forget
the frailties of human nature, forget that Seneca never claimed to
be the self-sufficient ideal Stoic sage.[23] Indeed, they forget what
Seneca himself had always insisted: that all human beings are
mad—*dementissimi*—(*Ep.* 70.3); that all men are flawed—*peccavimus omnes*—(*De Clem.* 1.6.3); and that the Stoic sage in his
perfection is a *rara avis*, appearing perhaps only once every five
hundred years (*Ep.* 42.1).

Since Seneca acknowledged human weakness in general and his
own in particular, we should accept the *Ad Polybium* as a work

composed under duress in moments of despair—a work which obviously our author later on would have regretted writing. Yet critics have taken two extreme positions regarding this Dialogue. As has been pointed out, his opponents utterly condemn him for writing it. His admirers, on the other hand, either deny Senecan authorship (as did Diderot)[24] or argue that it is a cunning piece of irony.[25] Since such hypotheses, however, have no solid foundation but rest on mere conjecture, we deem it preferable to conclude that the *Ad Polybium* was indeed written by Seneca[26] as an appeal to Claudius for deliverance from exile. Though he hoped that this treatise would win his recall, it by no means accomplished this goal. Another five years of his life were spent in Corsica before his release.

IV   *Recall from Exile*

Such release eventually came through revolutionary changes at the imperial court. Messalina, who continued to be, over the years, debased and reckless, was responsible for the murder of one person after another including Polybius in 47,[27] to whom Seneca had addressed the Consolation. Utterly debauched and overcome by passion for her lover Silius, she entered into a conspiracy with him which involved their matrimony during Claudius' absence in Ostia. An elaborate wedding ceremony took place, and the marriage was consummated. Silius then was to seize the sovereign power. Claudius' influential freedmen—Narcissus, Callistus, and Pallas—who in the past had been Messalina's accomplices, became alarmed by the destruction of Polybius, who had been a freedman like themselves, and by this outrageous marriage. Believing that their own position and power were now in jeopardy, they formed a conspiracy against the empress with Narcissus as leader. Messalina was denounced to the emperor. She and Silius were put to death the same night in the middle of autumn 48.[28]

Although Claudius vowed before the assembly of praetorian guards never to marry again, he quickly changed his mind and was soon in quest of another mate. Agrippina, daughter of Claudius' brother Germanicus, triumphed over other rivals and contracted an incestuous marriage with her uncle.[29] She further strengthened her position by betrothing Domitius, her twelve-year-old son by Ahenobarbus, to the young child Octavia, Claudius' daughter by Messalina. Moreover, Domitius was adopted by the Emperor under the name of Nero and elevated to a level with Britannicus, Claudius' and Messalina's nine-year-old son.[30]

Claudius, again, as in the past, allowed himself to be dominated by a woman. In fact, Agrippina's monopoly of power was so immense that, as René Waltz has observed, "Le règne de Claude est fini. La régence d'Agrippine commence."[31] Her aim was to oust Britannicus, rightful heir to the throne, to make Nero king, and through him to gain for herself supreme control. In pursuit of her goal, she decided, both for her own personal gains and perhaps too out of sympathy for a long-time friend of her family, to recall from exile Lucius Annaeus Seneca. For Seneca's name, after all, still retained a distinguished literary, philosophical, and moral reputation. Moreover, he had been far distant from the depravity and intrigue that had characterized Claudius' years in power. By reintroducing such an orator and statesman upon the scene, Agrippina certainly intended to win popularity for herself and to have the youthful Nero receive superior training in oratory and in government. Thus in 49, after eight years in Corsica, at the age of fifty-three, Seneca returned to Rome to become Nero's tutor. In addition to this responsibility, Agrippina, regarding him as an able political adviser, obtained for him the praetorship and placed him in the Senate.[32] So Seneca came once more to play an active role in Imperial Rome.

It was undoubtedly about this time that the philosopher married again. Of his second wife, Pompeia Paulina, much younger than himself, Seneca speaks in most tender terms, emphasizing their intense devotion to each other (*Ep.* 104.2–5). And Tacitus records with admiration and sympathy Paulina's fidelity to her beloved husband through the trials and tribulations of the Neronian Age.[33]

When Seneca accepted Agrippina's terms for recall from exile, he realized that neither educating Nero nor dealing with the new empress would be devoid of difficulty or danger. Assuredly he would have preferred to return to Rome without such burdensome involvement, to have spent his regained freedom in study and in the company of family and friends. He also would have enjoyed going to Athens.[34] But Seneca had no choice. He had to become Nero's tutor, he had to accept the praetorship, if he were to recover his liberty. Thus Seneca, like many a protagonist of Greek tragedy, was captive in a web of circumstance that whisked him from exile to the inner sanctum of empire. It is almost as if he perceived that there was no turning back, while he also understood well enough that the course he traveled was worse than perilous. The author of the pseudo-Senecan drama, *Octavia*, has a Seneca on stage acknowledge just such a tragic dilemma in the court: "O powerful Fortune, with false, flattering face,/ why have you exalted me, content with my lot, on high?/ That, from this elevated post, I might behold so many fears/ and the more heavily fall?" (*Octavia* 377–380).

It was under such circumstances that Seneca found himself playing a dominant political role from which there was no escape. All he could do was reconcile himself to the task before him and endeavor to play his part to the best of his ability—and to play it to the end.

Although Seneca realized the inhumane and ruthless nature of his young pupil,[35] he nevertheless devoted much energy attempting to inculcate in Nero humane principles, hoping that sound moral instruction might mollify his cruel tendencies. But Seneca was hindered in his efforts by Agrippina, who looked with disdain upon philosophic studies, warning her son that such pursuits were harmful to one destined to rule.[36] Seneca, therefore, had to confine his instruction principally to rhetoric and proper etiquette.[37]

To assist Seneca in educating the prince, Agrippina appointed for her son another tutor, Burrus, renowned for his intelligence, honesty, and courage, a soldier elevated by the empress to the rank of prefect of the praetorian guard. It was Agrippina's hope that, under the tutelage of these two outstanding men, Nero would become a skilled orator, an accomplished leader.

Though of diverse temperaments—Burrus, soldierly and austere, Seneca, gracious and gallant—these two men experienced an unusual, harmonious relationship rarely found where power is shared. Their friendship grew stronger day by day as they united in restraining Nero's excess and in circumscribing Agrippina's lawless spirit.[38]

Thus was Seneca restored to the tumultuous world of Roman politics and society; yet it was precisely such a climate of metropolitan commitment that confirmed Seneca's conviction that the life of solitude and thought *must be* integrated with the life of activity. Incontestably, the dynamic and dramatic role he played in this critical period in Roman history constitutes a singular memorial to a philosopher devoted to the concrete, the societal, the humane.

His service, however, was repeatedly disrupted and foiled. By 54, Agrippina was overcome with lust for power and infuriated by Claudius' affection for his son Britannicus who she dreaded would be proclaimed heir to the throne. At an opportune moment, she assassinated the emperor, serving him a dish of poisoned mushrooms.[39] His death was concealed until all arrangements were made for Nero's succession. Britannicus and his sisters were confined to their rooms. The senate was convened on the false news of the emperor's illness. Formal prayers were offered for his safety. Finally, at noon, on October 13, the palace gates were suddenly swung open, and Nero, accompanied by Burrus, advanced to the cohort on guard at the palace. Then, after a signal had been given by the prefect, Nero was greeted with shouts of joy and escorted by Burrus to the camp. Here, after delivering a speech to the soldiers composed by Seneca promising them a generous donative, he was saluted *Imperator*. The soldiers' pronouncement was followed by a decree of the Senate, and the provinces approved the choice without hesitation.[40]

Divine honors were voted to Claudius; since the time of Augustus, the custom had been established of "conferring" divinity upon a deceased ruler. Needless to say, in Claudius' case, this ceremonial was perfunctory. He had certainly not been a popular emperor. His slavishness to his wives, his cruelty, his absentmindedness, his love of gambling, and his inelegent stutter had hardly endeared his memory to the crowd. But the ceremonials were carried out. On the day of Claudius' funeral, Nero delivered an encomium, written by Seneca, to suit the occasion.[41] After praising Claudius' family, his learning, and the state's suffering no misery at the hands of barbarians during his reign (all factually true), the oration then celebrated with noticeable hyperbole the emperor's "wisdom" and "foresight." Tacitus almost gleefully reports that at that moment the audience was convulsed with laughter—adding that Seneca's wit was remarkably well suited to his era.

Equally amusing to the audience of his day must have been the pamphlet, introduced in the MSS. as *Ludus de morte Claudii Caesaris* or *Divi Claudii . . . Apotheosis Annei Senece per satiram*. This witty fiction, most frequently attributed to Seneca, appeared shortly after the official deification and is entitled by Dio Cassius the *Apocolocyntosis*[42]—commonly translated the "Pumpkinification" of Claudius. Obviously a parody mocking the ceremony which apotheosized the emperor and translated him to heaven, Seneca's ribald and wittily original satire translates the lame and stammering Claudius to hell. There, this emperor, the notoriously false judge, murderer, and idolater of trials during his lifetime, is appropriately made a mere underling court-clerk and consigned to rattling dice in a bottomless box—recalling the underworld fate of the murderous Danaides, who must forever draw water from a well in sieves. There is no reason for the reader to be surprised that Seneca wrote such a satire at such a time. As has been mentioned, Claudius was by no means a well liked and respected sovereign. Seneca, the artist, used this opportunity to create an original satire—one which he knew his fellow Romans would enjoy. Nor must the reader be surprised that Seneca devised the *laudatio funebris* for the young Nero; as Nero's tutor and guardian, Seneca frequently composed Nero's addresses—prior to Claudius' death as well as after Nero's accession to the throne.

Moreover, the role played by both tutors—Seneca and Burrus—was, at this time, natural and inevitable. No evidence indicates that either man knew anything of the secret plot for Claudius' assassination, and there is little advantage to be obtained by imagining otherwise. Yet, it must certainly be perceived that two substantially forthright and distinguished men were slowly becoming hopelessly entangled in Agrippina's dark web of conspiracy and ambition.

V *The* Quinquennium Neronis

Seneca, now, in the words of René Waltz, "marche à de nouveaux malheurs, mais par une voie glorieuse où il se signalera par les plus éminents services. . . ."[43]

For five years, from the accession of the seventeen-year-old Nero in 54 until 59—a period known as the *Quinquennium Neronis*—Seneca, with the aid of Burrus, restrained Nero's excesses and endeavored to instill in him justice and clemency.[44] In the *De Clementia*, written at this time specifically for Nero's instruction, Seneca urges a spirit of broad-mindedness. tolerance, *humanitas* toward one's fellow men. Dramatically in this treatise, the philosopher portrays the young ruler as saying: "With me the sword is hidden, indeed, it is buried in its sheath; I show mercy even to the basest of men; every man, though he lack all else, shall find favor with me because he is a human being. Severity I keep concealed; clemency ready at hand" (*De Clem.* 1.1.3–4).

The virtues of equity and kindness that characterized the early years of Nero's reign have rightfully been attributed to the unusual administration of Seneca and Burrus. Even Dio, so often adverse to Seneca, admits that the philosopher and prefect of the guard governed affairs so ably and justly that they won the praise of all men.[45] And the Emperor Trajan, a stern critic, proclaimed the Quinquennium Neronis the golden age of imperial Rome.[46]

The policies initiating this ideal period were announced to the Senate in a speech composed by Seneca and delivered by Nero immediately after Claudius' apotheosis. Nero assured the Senate that he, unlike Claudius, would not interfere with the legal system nor serve as judge in every case. The Senate and the consuls were, in fact, in his principate, to regain and retain considerable rights and responsibilities. The Senate was jubilant.[47]

Agrippina, however, who coveted for herself supreme control, annoyed by such reforms and by an administration founded on justice and humanity, became hostile to Seneca and Burrus. Filled with hate and in fear of losing her power, she threatened to give the throne to Britannicus, Claudius' genuine heir, and scathingly denounced "the demand of the cripple Burrus and the exile Seneca to rule the human race with deformed hand and professorial tongue."[48]

Agrippina's open support of the young prince filled Nero with dread and only served to hasten Britannicus' doom. At a dinner in the Imperial court, Britannicus was put to death by a poisonous drink served to him at the emperor's command. Agrippina, not anticipating this catastrophe, became all the more enraged and alarmed.[49] Seneca, "first in learning, first in power,"[50] was becoming more and more ensnared by the foul machinations of Agrippina and her son.

Agrippina had hoped that by recalling Seneca from exile he would ever have to remain conveniently and dutifully grateful to her. But, of course, she soon discovered that such was not to be the case. If Seneca was to retain the reins of a clement and beneficent government, he must naturally resist the petulant and vicious egoism of the young Nero on the one hand and the ravening ambition of his mother on the other. He was virtually the hapless mariner driven to steer in dangerous waters between Scylla and Charybdis.

And dangerous indeed was his course. After Britannicus' murder, the hostility between mother and son continued to mount. Nero deprived Agrippina of all her honors and of soldiers to guard her. He forbade her to reside in the palace. When he visited her in her new residence, he arrived surrounded by a throng of officers and departed after a terse greeting.[51]

Agrippina's enemies now saw their chance to take revenge on her for her ill treatment of them in the past. They accused her of forming a faction with the wealthy, powerful Rubellius Plautus, descendant, on his mother's side, of Augustus. According to them, Agrippina hoped to overthrow Nero, marry Plautus, and regain the power that she had exercised under Claudius. When this gossip was reported to the emperor by one of his favorites, Nero, drunk with wine, loudly determined to murder his mother and her accomplice. From such a deed, the frenzied Nero could only be deterred by direct interference of Seneca and Burrus. The two leaders in the state pleaded with the emperor, insisting that little or no direct evidence incriminated the mother, and urging that Nero at least give Agrippina a hearing. Thus for a time—but only for a brief time—the savage mother was spared by the savage son.[52] And as for Seneca, his appeals to "beneficence" and "clemency" were heard once again—but barely. It was becoming clear that Nero was actually declining into greater and greater depravity and unreason, and the philosopher could not expect to restrain this lunatic ruler very long.

Indeed Seneca was increasingly beset by the problem of Nero's extravagance, lewdness, and crime.[53] Moreover, the emperor was surrounded by unprincipled men, like Suillius, who, jealous of the philosopher's prestige and power, were determined to break his influence. Nero came more and more to rely upon such men, and, actuated by them, was eager to free himself from the precepts and restraints of his Stoic mentor.

About the same time, in 58, Seneca's position was further weakened by a rising power in court, an ominous female who displaced Nero's former mistress Acte. This new acquisition, whom Tacitus aptly describes as "a woman having everything but character," was none other than Poppaea Sabina, the wife of Otho—

one of Nero's own cronies.[54] Poppaea continually pressed the
emperor to rid himself not only of Seneca and Burrus but also
of his imperious mother, fully aware that, while Agrippina lived,
he would never divorce Octavia and marry his new mistress. And
she was right. Though he detested his mother, though he constantly scorned and abused her, he nevertheless always exhibited
in her presence a measure of awe and restraint, evidencing a
sullen compliance to her demands.[55] Now, however, under Poppaea's spell, he once and for all determined that he could only
be emancipated from Agrippina by her death.[56]

After several unsuccessful attempts to poison her, Nero next
embraced Anicetus' plan to drown her at sea. Though shipwrecked, she survived and succeeded in returning to her villa.
There could be no doubt that Agrippina now perceived the
treacheries afoot, and Nero, when he learned of this recently
fumbled attempt, became livid with hysterical fear. Apparently,
he expected "Mamma" to descend upon him and to thrash him
soundly. Like a child, he wildly envisioned Agrippina converting
the army, swaying the senate, arousing the people against him.
And so the grim drama must continue ludicrously to be played
out.

In a panic, he summoned Seneca and Burrus to an "advisory"
meeting. Tacitus concedes that it was doubtful that, until this
time, the two serious elder statesmen had been privy to Nero's
wretched designs. Consequently, after they had been informed,
the philosopher and the military prefect sat long in silence. Matters had already been carried far beyond those bounds where discourse or admonition might have effectively served a salutary
purpose. The childish and maniacal emperor could no longer be
approached by reason or guidance. Quietly, Seneca almost ironically asked Burrus if the guard would commit such a crime; of
course, the answer was No, for Roman soldiers would find it un-
thinkable to murder a member of the Imperial line. Even this
implicit rebuke to the emperor concerning the degree of his dishonor had no effect, and Burrus could only maintain that, if
Anicetus had devised such a crime, why, then, Anicetus must
carry it out. And so he did. He and two accomplices broke into
Agrippina's villa, entered her bedroom, and bludgeoned her to
death with club and sword.[57]

At this point, even Nero began to be fearful of the deed. In any event, he was, from his rural court in Campania, apprehensive of senatorial and public opinion back at Rome. Some trifling attempt, just prior to her murder, had been made to render Agrippina's death palatable. It was claimed that Agerinus, one of Agrippina's servants, had been sent to an audience with Nero, and was discovered armed with a dagger, and bent upon treachery at the direction of his mistress. He was dispatched, and Agrippina, it was alleged, in an excess of guilt feeling and self-recrimination for such treason, had taken her own life.[58]

But the elaborately woven and contrived "plot" seemed palpably threadbare, even to the emperor, and he continued to tremble at the thought of his public image. In gloom, he removed from Baiae to Naples and lingered, uncertain when or how to return to Rome. Although his agents had spread the story of Agrippina's treachery, Nero still feared her popularity with the masses. He sent a letter to the senate, composed by Seneca, in which, after charging his mother with plotting against her son and with committing suicide on being discovered, he offered lengthy lists and compilations of Agrippina's crimes—throughout Nero's own reign and extending even back to the reign of Claudius. He reported the nearly fatal shipwreck as being virtually a "sign" of the gods' displeasure with his mother and concluded by labeling the Roman people "fortunate" still because of her demise.[59]

The antithetic, epigrammatic, elegant style of this letter obviously directed attention not to Nero, but to Seneca. Tacitus reports that the absurdity of an "accidental" shipwreck and of a single servant's being thought capable of bursting through armies at court to perpetrate an assassination of Nero moved the populace to blame Seneca for being an accessory to the emperor's crimes.[60] Yet it can hardly be true that Nero was very seriously or openly detected in his crime, for even Tacitus indicates, a page or so later, that Nero's return to Rome was celebrated by one and all as a kind of triumph.[61] Patently, the story of Nero's bare escape from villainy was generally credited, and in such a climate Seneca could hardly have been maligned.

Far more important for us is a consideration of Seneca himself. For in writing such a letter for Nero, if he did not lose esteem in the public eye at that time, he certainly did in Tacitus'. Moreover, this event in his public career has perhaps been more damaging, through the centuries, to his reputation than any other. Assuredly these are Seneca's darkest days in the Neronian court. What had commenced as a reign devoted to clemency and regulated by philosophy declined into vicious intrigue and matricide. And upon every politic occasion, Seneca must compose a letter, or devise a speech. That Seneca was considerably enmeshed in the toils of Imperial vice there can be no doubt. And there can likewise be no doubt that Seneca suffered acutely for his role in much of this business. He himself speaks feelingly of the sufferings one must endure from one's conscience after being involved in wrongdoing (*Ep.* 97. 14–16).

In Seneca's case, however, certain facts must be considered. We must remember that he fully endorsed Zeno's doctrine that man's duty was to serve men, that the Stoic must engage in public life unless prevented from doing so. Seneca himself concedes: "If the State is so corrupt that it cannot be aided, if it is overwhelmed by evils, the wise man will not struggle in vain nor will he devote himself to it when it is profitless to do so" (*De Otio* 3.3). We need only ask if the State, at this pass, was beyond help. The answer is unequivocally that it was not. Even Tacitus observes that, a little later, Seneca and Burrus could still restrain Nero in some of his vice and folly. And it is highly significant that Nero was moved at this time to recall a great host of men and women from exile and to display a "clemency" obviously directed by his philosophic counselor. Indeed, Nero was now engaging in a host of foolish pastimes—performing with the lute upon the stage, acting dramatic roles, indulging in vulgar displays of chariot-driving, fostering Greek games, and the like.[62] Tacitus considers such imperial "displays" as horrifyingly degrading of one's "honor" as is matricide. But Seneca clearly does not. His policy appears to tolerate (and perhaps even encourage) Nero in private follies and shows—so long as the State and the people are not molested and undone.

At one point, Tacitus dryly observes that the noble senator Thrasea Paetus, disgusted with Nero, in a silent gesture of defiance, quit the senate. But, claims the historian, Paetus in so doing had thus "endangered himself without initiating liberty for others."[63] Seneca makes no such empty gesture at this critical period, and he obviously is laboring mightily to serve as "a source of liberty to others." To be sure, the philosopher recognized well

that service to mankind is no easy obligation—but rather a perpetual and vigilant duty that one should perform: "The work of
a good citizen is never useless; when heard, when seen, by his
expression, by his nod . . . by his very deportment, he is useful"
(*De Tranq. An.* 4.6). And Seneca himself, in his time, perceived
that such service was arduous indeed, for he compares its pursuit to the perils of warfare: "though he has lost his hands, a man
can aid his country in battle by voicing the war cry and by
standing firm" (*De Tranq. An.* 4.5). Seneca as yet is in no such
extremity in Nero's court, but he comprehends grimly, distinctly
the nature and the dangers of such a conflict.

VI *Seneca's Political Decline and Retirement*

To this point, Seneca has been wounded but he is still fight-
ing. And he will continue to fight for another three years, while
Burrus, with whom he has enjoyed an unbroken friendship and
an unusual harmony in government, remains at his side. The
prefect of the guard continues to control the military force, the
philosopher continues to exercise influence in the *consilium*
among the ministers of State.

But the distinguished government service of these two extraordinary men was soon to end. When Burrus died in 62—
whether by illness or by poison at Nero's command remains
uncertain—and was replaced by the debauched and licentious
Tigellinus,[64] Seneca finally became convinced that he no longer
had a part to play in Rome's complicated drama of the Neronian
Age.

We will recall that Agrippina, earlier, had exercised an inordinate but ambivalent influence over the young Nero. Suetonius
reports that her nagging inspection into his every act and her
constant reprimands at one point drove Nero to feign a threat of
abdicating and of retiring to Rhodes.[65] And the alert Tacitus observes that at the moment of her death, Nero "surrendered himself to all his immoderate desires which, though barely restrained,
had been somewhat slackened by his reverence for his mother,
such as it was."[66]

But it is by no means true that, upon her demise, Nero was
completely free to plunge himself into every vice and folly. For
although he took to chariot-driving and to other idle, dishonorable activities, it must be remembered that between Agrippina's

death in 59 and Burrus' in 62 he continued to be somewhat controlled. Seneca and Burrus, clearly, in some way, continued the very role which they always shared with Agrippina, a fear of their displeasure checking Nero's extravagance. And their success was signal: for the first eight years of Nero's principate, 54–62, there was no indication of conflict between emperor and his senate. There were no executions (as there had been under Claudius) of numerous senators. Only later, in 62, was the law of *maiestas* again invoked, and numbers of senators were tried and convicted. Moreover, during this same period, 54–62, the public had even been able to accept the deaths of Britannicus and Agrippina without any show of force. It was only in 62, after Burrus' death and Seneca's retirement, when Nero attempted to put aside his wife Octavia, that there were outbursts of public disapproval.

If Seneca and Burrus had curtailed this restless Caesar in public affairs (if not private ones) until 62 and had held over him some means of restraint which had likewise been exercised by Agrippina, they, like her, were also heirs to Nero's ambivalence and hostility.[67] Just as Agrippina had eventually to pay for her influence with her life, so eventually must Seneca and Burrus. Burrus' death in 62 marks the end of the years of Nero's restraint. And it is significant that every source rather openly suggests that Burrus was the victim of Nero and poison.

Now, almost wholly at liberty, the emperor came more and more to rely upon infamous colleagues, like Tigellinus, and also esthetes, like Petronius,[68] who functioned as boon companions rather than as counselors. Such men envied Seneca, the single mainstay from an earlier period of decorum and civic order at court. They maligned him for his enormous wealth, his artistry and brilliant eloquence and assaulted his already tottering position of influence. Constantly disparaging the philosopher, they repeatedly urged the emperor, now a full-grown youth of twenty-five, to dismiss this childhood pedagogue and erstwhile minister. And Nero hardly required these incentives.

Seneca, on the other hand, was fully aware of these factions, intrigues, and campaigns against him. Moreover, ever mindful of Burrus' departure, of Nero's volatile temperament, and of the calumniators' undisputed influence with the emperor, the philosopher recognized that the time had at last arrived for his withdrawal from public life.[69]

Thus in the *De Otio*, probably written about 62, Seneca strikes a new note, insisting that man can, at any time, but especially in old age, and more so if he has rendered long service to the State, abandon the world of civic action for the contemplative life. But we must observe that the *De Otio*, like so many of his writings, is remarkably apolitical. Only between the lines are we able to discern the degree of the philosopher's disillusionment with Nero and with attempts to regulate the Roman State. Like Plato with Dionysius, Seneca comes face-to-face with garish realities that ravish a manly dream. "If that government," he obliquely writes, "which we envision cannot be found, withdrawal becomes a necessity" (*De Otio* 8.3).

Consequently, the philosopher at sixty-five, disappointed, saddened by a long, frustrating experience, dared to confront his former pupil to request retirement and release. This famous scene is important enough to receive meticulous delineation in Tacitus.[70] For Seneca fully realized, at this juncture, that one *cannot* petition retirement, or escape from this court. As one scholar well observes: "The truly new departure of Nero's absolutism consisted in this: not only opposition but also neutrality and retirement were no longer to be possible. Men were not at liberty to say nothing, as Cicero had asserted of Caesar; everyone had to support the autocrat actively."[71] Because of the futility and precariousness of Seneca's request, the dramatic scene in Tacitus crackles with tension. In his stateliest manner, nevertheless, Seneca forthrightly asks his emperor for permission to retire, so that he might devote the remainder of his life to studies. Moreover, with a bold stroke—being perfectly willing to annihilate envy and purchase freedom at the highest price—he offers to return to Nero the millions of his wealth that the emperor had once bestowed. Not without a touch of grim irony, he acknowledges that "Both of us have filled up the measure." Events have carried them to the Rubicon. And throughout, Seneca is remarkable for balance and unflinching control. In a taut style, typically Senecan, he says: "Both of us have filled up the measure: you, of all that a ruler could confer upon his friend; I, of all that a friend could accept from his ruler. . . . You have more than enough strength and you have observed for years how to exercise the highest power. We, your friends who are older, may demand our repose."[72]

With a malevolence lurking just beneath the surface, Nero replies in a style that reveals the rhetorical ease and cleverness taught to him by his erudite mentor. No, he counters. He could not possibly take back the gifts he bestowed on him, which may appear many but, in reality, are few when compared to the possessions held by men not at all comparable to Seneca in character. Furthermore, Seneca is *not* too old to continue to guide Nero's youth: "Why not go on recalling to the right path the slippery steps of my youth and guide even more vehemently that strength of mine adorned by your support." Nero's decision was followed with embraces and kisses; the confrontation was at an end. And Tacitus bitingly adds: "Seneca expressed his thanks— the usual manner for terminating a meeting with a tyrant."[73]

Nevertheless, if Seneca could not obtain the permission and actual fact of release, he boldly took measures to assume the posture of retirement for all practical purposes: he avoided the court and the city, avoided all factions and crowds, and commenced in earnest a life of self-exile, seclusion, and study. In reporting Burrus' death, Tacitus had commented that "with one of the two leaders gone, good government lost much of its force";[74] we must add that with Seneca's withdrawal from the political scene, good government was lost entirely.

Yet what the cause of civilization here lost in the political realm, it certainly gained in philosophy and literature. For these years of retirement, 62–65, constitute the *anni mirabiles* of Seneca's literary career. To them can be assigned with certainty his *maximum opus,* the 124 *Moral Letters (Epistulae Morales),* as well as the seven books of *Natural Questions (Quaestiones Naturales).* To this same fruitful period, scholars, involved in the insoluble problem of dating the Senecan corpus, have often attributed the seven books *On Benefits (De Beneficiis),* the dialogues *On Leisure (De Otio)* and *On Providence (De Providentia),* along with several other works.

Though ensconced in the tranquility of thought and composition, Seneca was nevertheless constantly harassed by an aura of impending doom. Since Nero had never officially released him from court, the shadow of imperial tyranny continued to haunt his retirement.

Most dreadful at this time (64) was the great fire. The destruction of Rome in the conflagration was believed to have been instigated by the emperor.[75] Nero, of course, fastened the blame upon the Christians and proceeded to slaughter thousands of the innocent with a reckless ferocity. Moreover, the maddened emperor, ever addicted to art and architecture, commenced the rebuilding of Rome with a frenzied extravagance—virtually bleeding all of the empire for funds and even ransacking the temples and shrines for valuables and gold. Tacitus claims that such an accumulation of evils (but especially the sacrilege) made it rumored abroad that Seneca again attempted to retire at a great distance from the court and the city, but that Nero again had refused. Thereupon, the philosopher feigned illness and confined himself to his bedroom, subsisting on the most meager diet, Tacitus affirms, of fountain water and fresh fruit—attempting to escape poisoning (the emperor's favorite method for dispatching kith and kin).[76]

VII *The Death of Seneca*

But neither concealment nor precaution could rescue Seneca from the bane of Nero's malevolence. By 65, three years after his attempted seclusion, Seneca's end was at hand. It appears that during this period Neronian incompetence, giddiness, and vice achieved a fullness of measure that was too considerable for many a citizen to bear. Thus was devised the so-called Pisonian Conspiracy involving dozens of aristocrats and people of every class[77]—a conspiracy that intended no less than the assassination of the emperor himself. But by a stroke of fickle good fortune, Nero became apprised of the intrigue a few hours before it could be perpetrated. A freedman of Scaevinus informed on the group, and many were haled to court, imprisoned, questioned. At the threat of torture, a number of the important accomplices broke down and "confessed." At that moment, Seneca's fate was sealed, for one of the principal confessors, Antonius Natalis, accused the philosopher of complicity in this Pisonian Conspiracy.

The plot had as its object the murder of Nero and the transfer of supreme power to Piso, or, as was rumored by some, to Seneca himself.[78] What role Nero's former teacher actually had played in this conspiracy remains uncertain. It is noteworthy, however, that, at the outset of his account of this plot, Tacitus lists in great detail the most prominent conspirators yet omits Seneca's name entirely.[79] It is only five or six chapters later, after Nero has become fully cognizant of the plot, that, in Natalis' confession, Seneca's name appears. Terrified and limp with fear, Natalis first implicates Gaius Piso, then names Annaeus Seneca. And Tacitus adds that perhaps Seneca was designated "to win favor with Nero, who, in his hostility to Seneca, sought every device to destroy him."[80] Indeed, Tacitus considers this interpretation important, for he repeats it later: "The elimination of Annaeus Seneca followed, an event most joyful to the emperor; not because he had any evidence of his complicity in the conspiracy, but that, since he had failed to kill him with poison, he might attack him with the sword."[81]

Seneca's active participation in such a cabal is cast further in doubt by the very nature of the "confessions." For once participants in the scheme were in custody, they all too unheroically blurted confessions in plenty, their name-dropping so vast and inclusive as to remind us of many of the so-called confessions of witches in New England; many a man obviously perished on both occasions without having had the benefit of the least information about the crime. Lucan, when confessing, first named his own mother; others, like Senecio, designated their best friends.[82]

Neverthless, if Seneca was innocent of actively engaging in this conspiracy, he could hardly have been ignorant of its existence and purport. As a friend to Piso, uncle to Lucan, and acquaintance to many of the other would-be liberators, he must certainly have obtained knowledge of the design. He had, after all, ever admired as an heroic exemplar, Cato the Younger, who during the Civil War of the preceding century became the pattern of armed resistance to tyranny. Of this ideal Stoic Seneca writes: "His entire life was passed either in civil war or on the verge of it. And it can be said, although surrounded by the slavish, he, no less than Socrates, devoted himself to liberty" (*Ep.* 104.29).[83] Seneca would hardly have frowned upon the virtue of "libertas." But it was not consistent with his temperament and behavior to encourage violence and anger. He doubtless remained true to his retirement and dedication to studies, while possibly wishing the adventurers well.

But guilty or innocent, Seneca had, in any event—as he well

knew—to confront the merciless fury of a maniacal ruler. He had to pay the debt of his life to an emperor who had much earlier determined upon the exaction and the price.

Natalis affirmed that when he had been sent by Piso to visit Seneca, who was ill, and to complain of too little intimacy between the philosopher and Piso, Seneca replied that "conversations with one another and frequent conferences were to the benefit of neither; but his own well-being depended on Piso's safety."[84] Nero then sent a tribune and soldiers to inquire of Seneca if the report were true. Coolly, Seneca admitted Natalis' visit but denied the reply Natalis had reported. As for his refusal to allow Piso to visit him, "he had excused himself because of his illness and his love of quiet." Furthermore, the philosopher continues, he would never concede that his life was dependent upon another's, nor would he ever display such servility; if anything, he had always been free and forthright in speech rather than servile, as Nero himself could attest.[85]

Yet Nero had found his opportunity and would not relinquish it. Like so many others implicated in the conspiracy, Seneca was instructed by military officers to commit suicide. Here we encounter one of the most famous scenes in antiquity—certainly one of the great deathbed performances of all time. Seneca received the sentence with a calm and notable dignity and straightway set about the business. The common method by which aristocrats did themselves in (the nobility was treated as being above the indignity of execution by another) was to sever an artery in the arm, and thereafter to settle back for a period of painful but respectable dis-ease, slowly bleeding to death. This was Seneca's case.

It is noteworthy that his wife Paulina insisted upon accompanying him, even though Seneca had at first opposed her. He subsequently relented, but, after they had been placed in different rooms, it is reported that Nero prevented her demise by binding her wound.

More significant is the fact that Seneca's own death was noble in the extreme, yet fraught with accidents and mischances throughout. Being an old man, he bled slowly, and his dying was cruelly protracted. Even additional bleeding from the legs did not accelerate his passing, nor, later, did the administration of poison. Finally, the philosopher ordered himself placed in a warm bath,

where the heat and fumes at last contributed to his expiration.[86]
Despite this complicated ordeal, Seneca certainly died with philosophical calm and distinction—never once faltering, ever poised
and polished, quite fully the Stoic that he had always striven to
become.

Indeed, true to his studies, Seneca remained almost super-
humanly dedicated to the intellectual life. Dio Cassius reports
that, in the very hours of his dying, he continued ceaselessly in
revising a book he had been writing, unwilling that a moment be
lost.[87] With slight variation, Tacitus claims that Seneca summoned
his secretaries, proceeding to dictate to them a lengthy discourse,
his last philosophic communication with the public.[88]

Most important of all is the "pattern" of Seneca's death. Seneca
certainly had the "ideals" of conduct at one's death to a large
degree from Zeno and other Stoic fathers. But his own response
to the final hours called to life in him other exemplars, other
patterns. We should understand, as Thomas Mann reminds, us
that

The Ego of antiquity and its consciousness of itself was different from
our own, less exclusive, less sharply defined. It was, as it were, open
behind; it received much from the past and by repeating it gave it
presentness again. The Spanish scholar Ortega y Gasset puts it that
the man of antiquity, before he did anything, took a step backwards.
. . . He searched the past for a pattern into which he might slip as
into a diving bell, and being thus at once disguised and protected
might rush upon his present problem. Thus his life was in a sense a
reanimation, an archaizing attitude. But it is just this life as reanimation that is the life as myth. Alexander walked in the footsteps of
Miltiades; the ancient biographers of Caesar were convinced, rightly
or wrongly, that he took Alexander as his prototype. But such "imitation" meant far more than we mean by the word today. It was a myth-
ical identification, peculiarly familiar to antiquity; but it is operative
far into modern times. . . .[89]

Most significant, of course, in these closing hours, is Seneca's
revivification of Socrates. No one, reading Tacitus' account of
Seneca's conduct, can fail to recollect Plato's master. The manner
in which Seneca expostulates with his friends, argues with, ad-
jures, and consoles them—together with his steady calm—must
recall the Socrates of the *Crito* and *Phaedo*. And no one should

fail to remark the event when Seneca, like Socrates, has recourse to hemlock.[90] Nor should one fail to recollect Seneca's other "master pattern" in conduct—Cato the Younger.[91]

As Seneca himself had observed: "long is the journey through precepts, short and effective through examples" (*Ep.* 6.5). And more particularly: "If still you want a model, take Socrates. . . . Do you wish another model? Take Marcus Cato, closer to our own times . . ." (*Ep.* 104.27, 29). And thus it was. At the point of his dying, Seneca not only mustered his own private courage for right conduct but also assembled the models and paragons of a lasting tradition. That double measure is, in fact, what we most frequently mean by the "classic."

Tacitus has left us a moving description of Seneca's last, classic, exemplary hours—detailing his courage in the face of death. Here, chiefly, is Seneca presented as recalling his sad friends from tears to fortitude by that very philosophy that had so strongly and for so long molded his own character. "Where," he asks his companions, "were the precepts of wisdom? Where was that rationality developed over the years to help us face adversity?" Thereafter, Seneca speaks on a more personal note: "Who was, after all, unfamiliar with Nero's cruelty? There was nothing left for one who had murdered his brother and his mother but to slaughter his teacher and guide."[92] Why should his friends be surprised? Rather, they should accept the predictable and continue to regulate their lives despite the evils and mischances present in this world. Seneca himself, it is implied, had pursued such a pattern: he had directed his pinnace in open seas and political waters when that was possible, and he had steadied his craft in studious streams and standing pools when that was possible. No such life, successful upon the various tides, could possibly have been in vain.

Forbidden, as Tacitus details, to make his last will, Seneca turns to his friends and observes that, prevented from rewarding their merit in the public coin, he could only leave to them his "richest" possession—"the image of his life."[93] And we are meant to be left in no doubt but that this "private coin" is indeed the vast wealth of Socratic, Catonian, and Stoic tradition. Such was his generous legacy to posterity.

CHAPTER 2

The Opulent Stoic on Trial

THOUGH distinguished men in all ages have drawn heavily upon the Senecan legacy and have been sensible of the philosopher's munificence, there have been, nevertheless, a number of censurers who cannot forgive him for his affluence. Such critics have devoted their efforts to expounding the inconsistencies between Seneca's actions and his words, without presenting any concrete evidence for such a view. Hypotheses, conjectures, and suppositions of widest extent uttered in baffling generalities, without specific references to the philosopher's writings, form the bulk of their indictment. In support of their imaginative theses, they cite Dio Cassius as final authority, though somehow they have never been motivated to investigate Dio's source or to evaluate his statements truly.

Among the many charges brought against Seneca and recurring from century to century is the crucial one condemning his monetary hypocrisy. To these detractors, Seneca epitomizes the Stoic teacher whose preaching is controverted by practice; for them, here is the millionaire philosopher, bawling for poverty.

That Seneca amassed an enormous fortune is attested by several ancient sources.[1] Juvenal refers to him as *praedives,* "very rich,"[2] and the philosopher himself in his writings is not reticent about his own great wealth. So large and numerous were his villas and gardens that they were said to rival those of the emperor Nero.[3]

It is unfortunately true that immense fortune gives rise to immense suspicion. Even a man of most upright character is often suspected of dishonesty if he possesses extraordinary wealth. The philosopher who preaches his doctrine in shabby cloak with unkempt hair is more apt to be respected by his fellow men than the one who glitters amidst prosperity and power.[4] Oddly enough, opposition to Seneca's wealth is expressed even by one critic who is willing to acknowledge that Seneca's riches were honorably acquired.[5] Is it not, then, wealth per se that such a critic is condemning?

I *The Prosecution*

No great effort need be expended in discovering the origin and source of the charges that have circulated against Seneca down through the ages. According to Tacitus,[6] these accusations were first promulgated in 58 by one P. Suillius, who became angered by the revival of the Cincian Law, which forbade advocates to plead for pay. Feeling that Seneca, as Nero's minister, was the prime mover in this endeavor to constrain him personally, Suillius therefore launched a fierce attack against the philosopher-statesman, assailing him as foe to all the friends of Claudius. His assault contained these charges:

(1) The bookworm Seneca, who had spent his time in idle studies and in the company of inexperienced juveniles, naturally envied those who (like Suillius) served the public, and the larger, good.

(2) In the reign of Claudius, while Suillius nobly served Germanicus as *quaestor,* Seneca was seducing Germanicus' daughter.

(3) Could Suillius' humble acceptance of a grateful client's fee possibly equal Seneca's defilement of an imperial princess?

(4) Moreover, what philosophy, what intellectual genius had spurred Seneca. within the span of a mere four years, to amass 300,000,000 sesterces ($30,000,000)? And why had so many testaments irresistibly been drawn his favor? What doctrine inspired him to lend money to Italy and the provinces at such exorbitant interest?

These accusations, Suillius hoped, would break Seneca's power and influence.[7] Suillius was right; within the year, Seneca was made to discover the ominous effects of these very attacks,[8] ill effects that were to increase steadily throughout his lifetime, that, in fact, were ultimately to cut this life short. And still, Suillius' success was not done; it was larger than this—larger, doubtless, than even *he* could have dared to suspect. For, curiously enough, in the long, unfolding panorama of almost two thousand years of history, Suillius' bold wish has been repeatedly granted.

By 200, we find Dio Cassius (or his epitomizer Xiphilinus) transmitting these same accusations, embellished, however, by more striking exaggeration and more lively gossip. Here, in essence, are his recriminations:

(1) Seneca was not merely the seducer of the poor Julia, Germanicus' daughter; he was a flagrant seeker after young boys as well. Also, he was the adulterer with Nero's own mother.[9]

(2) Although ever criticizing the wealthy, Seneca was most busy amassing 300,000,000 sesterces; moreover, he absolutely required the possession of five hundred citrus wood tables, while, in addition, each and every one of these tables stood upon ivory legs; and with them all he served banquets.[10]

(3) Seneca's usury not only drained the provinces but also incited a rebellion in all of Britain. He had forced upon the misfortunate islanders 40,000,000 sesterces, money that these people in fact did not want; then with the most sudden harshness recalled his loan in its entirety.[11]

And so this singular line of criticism develops, extending down to our own day:

1670: John Milton:

. . . Seneca, in his books a philosopher, having drawn the Britons unwillingly to borrow of him vast sums upon fair promises of easy loan, and for repayment take their own time, on a sudden compels them to pay in all at once with great extortion. Thus provked [sic] by heaviest suffering . . . the Icenians . . . rise up in arms.[12]

1837: Thomas B. Macaulay:

The business of a philosopher [like Seneca] was to declaim in praise of poverty with two millions sterling out at usury, to meditate epigrammatic conceits about the evils of luxury, in gardens which moved the envy of sovereigns.[13]

1874: F. W. Farrar:

And in Seneca we see some of the most glowing pictures of the nobility of poverty combined with the most questionable avidity in the pursuit of wealth. . . . Inconsistency is written on the entire history of his life, and it has earned him the scathing contempt with which many writers have treated his memory.[14]

1887: C. T. Cruttwell:

He . . . in the short space of four years amassed an enormous fortune.
. . . Seneca is a lamentable instance of variance between precept and
example.[15]

1936: H. J. Rose:

Of [Seneca's] works the writer finds it hard to judge fairly, owing to
the loathing which his personality excites. . . . [When such a man]
takes the tone of a rigid moralist and a seeker after uncompromising
virtue, preaching, from his palace, simplicity and the plainest living
with almost the unction of a St. Francis praising Holy Poverty . . . the
gorge of the reader rises and he turns for relief to someone who either
made his life fit his doctrine or, if he behaved unworthily of the best
that was in him, at least laid no claim to be a spiritual guide.[16]

1955: Harry E. Wedeck:

One of the most provocative features in the Epistulae Morales of Lucius Annaeus Seneca is the flagrant discrepancy between his precepts,
in regard to wealth and poverty, on the one hand, and, on the other,
his manifest disregard, if not defiance, of these precepts in his accumulation of vast riches. . . . We must, therefore, taking into consideration
all the factual testimony, conclude that Seneca's contempt for wealth
cannot be reconciled with his acquisition of wealth.[17]

Upon such a long, persistent line of criticism rests the case against
Seneca and his wealth.

II   *The Defense*

In any defense of Seneca, we must, if we are to judge fairly,
cross-examine the original plaintiff. Since we have seen that this
host of critics is merely re-echoing the original charges, our concern is naturally not with these men. We must return to P. Suillius
himself. What became of him after he made his accusations
against Seneca? He himself was tried. Against this man it was
easy for Seneca and his powerful followers to present a case.
They, in their turn, promptly countercharged that Suillius had
plundered the provincials and embezzled public moneys during

his quaestorship in Asia. Since, however, these charges of criminality abroad would have required at least a year for investigation, it was decided to try him for crimes at home. Witnesses were found to testify against Suillius for numerous deaths which he had caused during the reign of Claudius. Suillius pleaded that he had engaged in those crimes in obedience to the emperor. But when Nero alleged that the notes of his adoptive father contained no such orders, Suillius was forced to shift his ground and to impute the guilt to Claudius' wife, Messalina. It was decided that he who had received pay for these crimes should now pay his due penalty. He was convicted, deprived of part of his fortune, and banished to the Balearic Isles. He was said to have enjoyed a life of luxury and comfort there.[18]

Was this man unfairly judged? Had he been made to fall, innocent victim of the wealthy Seneca? Or was his mild Balearic fate justly earned? Who was this Publius Suillius? If we are to follow the unprejudiced account of Tacitus himself,[19] we discover the answer in full. The historian describes him as a *delator*, as *terribilis ac venalis,* a man who had earned the hatred of many;[20] a pitiless, purchasable spy, devoid of morality, who earned his living and, in fact, enriched himself by making accusations against eminent men of his day.[21] Is it upon this base foundation, then, that an edifice of twenty centuries of Senecan prosecution has been built?

It is unfortunate that there is preserved no other contemporary report of Seneca's life.[22] The work of Fabius Rusticus, contemporary historian and friend of Seneca, who defended the philosopher against those very charges of Suillius, has not survived.[23] We are therefore left with no contemporary record of Seneca's life, save for the desperate opinion of this Publius Suillius. Think of the barren image we should have of Socrates, had the works of Plato and Xenophon not come down to us and were we wholly dependent upon Aristophanes' description of this Athenian philosopher. To be sure, we should have a highly distorted, misconstrued view. Such is the view left to us of Seneca, if we were to rely upon Suillius alone.

Certainly we can accept none of Suillius' charges as verified fact. It is impossible, in reality, to determine the exact amount of Seneca's wealth[24] or to know the exact means by which it was accumulated. Likewise, we cannot know that Seneca enhanced his wealth in any way by cunning or dishonor; the allegations affirming his legacy-hunting and enormous usury can never be credited with the least validity.[25] Honor and honesty must restrain us from rendering a verdict upon these grounds.

We can, of course, establish that Seneca possessed wealth. This was common knowledge. Since he came from a family of wealth and distinction, he naturally inherited much of his fortune. In the *Ad Helviam* (14.3), he praises the care and wisdom with which his mother managed the rich inheritances of her sons.

Furthermore, this inherited wealth was doubtless augmented by Seneca's renowned oratory; so successful and popular an advocate was he that he aroused the envy of Caligula himself.[26] His riches, too, were all the more increased by generous gifts bestowed upon him by the emperor Nero.[27] Although we have no record of it, yet it was possible, too, that he lent portions of this wealth to others, receiving some rate of interest for this service. Such is the common practice, we realize, in every culture, in every civilization that we might choose to study—including our own.

Thus we prove, beyond doubt, that Seneca possessed great wealth. But can we condemn him on this count alone? Indeed we cannot: it will have to be shown that wealth was inconsistent with Seneca's ideals; it will have to be shown that he has falsified his teaching by his actual conduct. This would finally score his hypocrisy.

Before giving our verdict in this matter, it is therefore most essential that we call our last and most important witness concerning any such hypocrisy between word and deed—Lucius Annaeus Seneca himself.

In the *De Vita Beata* (23.1), composed in 58, for the purpose of defending himself against Suillius' charges, Seneca writes: "The philosopher will possess ample wealth but it will have been wrested from no one nor stained with another's blood; it will have been acquired without wrong done to anyone, without resorting to base sources of gain; the expenditure of it will be as honorable as was its acquisition; it will cause no man to groan except the malicious."

Critics who have put their trust in the slander of Suillius and Dio either must have been unfamiliar with this passage or else were more prone to believe a *delator* and an unreliable historian than a distinguished philosopher and statesman whose precepts have occasioned a persistent influence upon the great minds of every century.[28]

Moreover, the works of Seneca abound in references to wealth and poverty. As a Stoic philosopher, he naturally classifies them among the "indifferent" things—things that lie outside the categories of the sole good and the sole evil,[29] since only that which is absolutely good, or *virtus,* can be considered a good, and only that which is absolutely bad, or *turpitudo,* can be considered an evil.[30] Among the "indifferent" things some (e.g., health and riches) are advantages, while others (e.g., poverty and disease) are disadvantages. So Seneca writes: "Moreover, who among wise men of our school, who regard virtue as the highest good, denies that even those things which we call 'indifferent' have some intrinsic worth and that some are preferable to others. . . . Do not therefore be deceived—wealth is among the more desirable things."[31]

The wise man, Seneca argues, finds in riches, rather than in poverty, greater opportunity to display his liberality, diligence, and magnanimity (*De Vita Beata* 22.1). Indeed there is no danger attaching to a man's possession of even extraordinary riches, provided he remains sufficiently detached from them (*De Vita Beata* 20.3; *Ep.* 5.6), realizing that fickle Fortune not only brings gifts but takes them away as well.[32] To those adverse critics more vituperative than informed, it must be pointed out that this is Seneca's basic meaning when he frequently refers to scorn of wealth.[33]

That Seneca scorned wealth and yet himself was wealthy is true. But he wore the gifts of Fortune gracefully, without being possessed by them (*Ad Helv.* 5.3–6; 10.2). And, significantly, it may be said that this guide of mankind, this preacher of humanitarianism, put his wealth into use, his philosophy into practice. Sound evidence of Seneca's generosity is, in fact, guaranteed by both Juvenal[34] and Martial.[35]

On this note, the defense of the accused must rest. Concerning the charges plied against Seneca and his wealth, any court can render but one resounding verdict: Not guilty; case dismissed.

CHAPTER 3

The Keystones of Senecan Philosophy

I   The Progress of the Soul

IN his philosophic writings, Seneca is certainly no romantic idealist; life in the Neronian era would hardly have encouraged fancy and transcendence. Rather, his view of society is pragmatic and austere. The mass of men, Seneca holds, are irresolute, ambitious, greedy, and impious.[1] Human life too often resembles the base struggle of wild beasts, men all too ready and eager to destroy one another in their mad and selfish pursuit of booty flung by fortune into their midst (*Ep.* 74.8–9; *De Ira* 2.8). In any crowded place—in the forum, say, or the circus—one will encounter a collection of as many vices as there are men (*De Ira* 2.8.1; *Ep.* 7.2–3). Human nature departed long ago from the peace, happiness, and innocence of the Golden Age, when men lived together in societies free of corruption and depravity. On the contrary, life as we know it resembles a terrestrial inferno (*Ep.* 90.38; *De Ira* 2.9).

Nevertheless, the spectacle of universal depravity should not cause us to despise our fellow men. The wise man, Seneca argues, will not be the opponent but the reformer of vice (*De Ira* 2.10.7; *De Vita Beata* 26.5). He will look upon the masses with tolerance, viewing them as sick men in need of a physician (*De Cons. Sap.* 13.1–3; *De Ira* 2.10.7–8). Nor does Seneca foolishly exempt himself from this base condition (*De Vita Beata* 17.3–4; 18.1–2; *Ad Helv.* 5.2); in private *and* in public life all men are mad—*non privatim solum sed publice furimus* (*Ep.* 95.30); all men are evil —*omnes mali sumus* (*De Ira* 3.26.4; cf. *De Benef.* 1.10.3). With such profound insight into human failings, Seneca nonetheless attempts a remedy. His writings display an urgency, an anxiety to raise the moral tone of mankind; his *Dialogues* reveal incessant quarrel and debate that seek to foster reform.

49

For Seneca is committed to belief in the possibility of moral progress in men. He does not despair even of the man who has plunged into the worst habits (*De Benef.* 7.19.5). Believing each individual to have the divine seed of virtue in him, he is hopeful that advice, guidance, and cultivation will stir it into growth (*Ep.* 94.29; 108.8). He is therefore eager to present man with the tools and principles that will serve him as a rule of life.

Man's essence, Seneca holds, is twofold: he possesses a physical nature which he shares with the other animals, and a rational nature which is his distinguishing mark, the quality possessed by him alone.[2] By virtue of this rational faculty man may claim relationship with eternal reason, that force governing the universe. In life, each creature pursues what is most suited to its nature: nothing else can have real value for it. Such a creature is in harmony with its own nature when it is governed by its own ruling principle, a beast by its animal mentality, and a man by his reason.[3]

Since the ruling principle in man is his reason, the well-being of his life depends upon rational action or, in other words, in the synchronization of himself and divine reason in the universe in a perfect harmony.

Hence every individual rises or falls on the scale of humanity and happiness as he succeeds or fails in harmonizing his actions with nature and reason. Only when his ruling principle is freely operating is it well with man; when that is the case, he may be said to possess "virtue" (*Ep.* 76.10). Such virtue is indeed man's sole and supreme good, and happiness consists exclusively in virtue.[4] Only that which is absolutely good (or *virtus*) can be considered a good, and only that which is absolutely bad (or *turpitudo*) can be considered an evil (*De Benef.* 7.2.2; *De Vita Beata* 4.3). Such was the traditional Stoic teaching, which further distinguishes all things which lie outside the categories of good and evil as being *indifferentia* (*Ep.* 82.10; *De Benef.* 1.6.2). Among such "indifferent things," it is true, some (health and riches) are advantageous, while others (poverty and disease) are disadvantageous (*Ep.* 74.17; *De Vita Beata* 22.4). However desirable or influential the former may be, yet Seneca and the Stoic school sharply distinguish between their purely relative value and the absolute value of virtue (*Ep.* 74.17; 92.19).

For virtue is conceived as flawless, self-sufficient, perfect (*Ep.* 74.12). Because virtue is one thing, and not many, it offers man a unified perception of the good and renders his life consistent, whole (*Ep.* 74.30). Hence, the happiness that such virtue affords can be neither increased nor diminished by extraneous conditions and indifferent things (*Ep.* 66.9; 74.24, 26; 92.14).

The follies, errors, and sins of men spring from unreason; men grasp the faulty notion of the good, fostered by a greedy desire for external things that are dependent on Fortune (*Ep.* 8.3). The avaricious, the sensual, and the worldly often estimate many insignificant things as important for want of understanding. They pursue false and fickle objects of desire that have no abiding goodness, bear no relation to man's moral nature, have not that unconditional value which alone should be esteemed. Happiness is not to be found in riches, power, or the pleasure of the senses—gifts of fortune that are flashy, fleeting, deceptive—but in the untainted and rational mind. Were anything nonrational, anything not contained in the individual soul, capable of determining man's happiness, man would be the victim of external forces, prevented from ever obtaining self-control. In such a climate, virtue (a word based upon *vir*, i.e., "man") would be meaningless and peace of mind impossible. But this is *not* the case; man is capable of self-regulation, of attaining to wisdom. And the wise man will detach himself from fickle Fortune's material gifts. He must regard them, rather, as household furniture, lent to him, which can be capriciously withdrawn (*Ad Marc.* 10.1; cf. *De Vita Beata* 3.3).

Because man is self-determining, he *does* possess the capacity to change, to learn virtue and wisdom. And once he has achieved independence of the whims of chance, man *has* become wise, *has* become completely free and happy (*Ep.* 59.16). Attaining to such a state, a profound peace then fills the wise man's soul, which external conditions can neither elevate nor depress.[5] In this condition, his calm and unchanging mental disposition has forever transcended the throbs of anxiety and fear, the flutterings of desire—those central causes of spiritual unrest. Free from disquietude, the newly initiated wise man enjoys a liberty and serenity of mind that are unalterable. Since his happiness is internally acquired, so it can never be destroyed by external forces (*Ep.* 72.8; *De Cons. Sap.* 9.3). Naturally, the reformation that produces such tranquillity is man's own spark of divine reason. Any man who grooms and nourishes his reason may secure some degree of virtue.

Consequently, Seneca and the Stoics tenaciously maintain that virtue can be obtained (*Ep.* 123.16). Since rational control and virtue are the same, and since children are not possessed of reason (*Ep.* 121.14; *De Benef.* 3.31.2), it follows that virtue is acquired, not by nature but by art, not by inheritance, but by labor and instruction (*De Ira* 2.10.6). Those who are imperfect need not despair; they should continue to persevere, confident that by training they will daily approach the nearer to their goal (*Ep.* 34.3; 71.36).

Thus, man must acquire the art of wisdom; he must progress from childish ignorance to the acquisition of responsible and manly virtue. It is no accident that Seneca's prose is filled with the metaphor viewing man's life as a journey;[6] he conceives of man's road as one requiring motion, alteration, accomplishment. And any subject in which all men partake may, as Aristotle had observed, be organized as an "art" and treated systematically.[7] Since all must travel from ignorance to knowledge, the learned and the humanitarian must produce maps to direct man on his way. For this reason Seneca appears constantly in his philosophical writings as a "guide" to travelers, as traffic director. Both in his studies and in the court of Nero, he had acquired a profound knowledge of human sorrow, ignorance, and aspiration, and sought to supply traveling men with rules of the road; for sickened men he wished to provide some medicine and relief for the soul. Throughout his philosophic prose, he displays an ardent, personal passion to enlighten pilgrims, to ease men in their peregrination, and to share knowledge of the highroad to virtue and happiness. "Nothing can ever delight me, however extraordinary and beneficial, if I must keep it to myself. If wisdom were given to me on condition that I conceal it with reticence, I should refuse. It is no pleasure to possess any good, without a friend to share it."[8]

In his works, the philosopher's aim is consistently directed toward edification. Of the three branches of ancient philosophy—ethics, physics, and dialectic—it is with the first two that Seneca is concerned. The last he regards as too often an empty and dangerous study, consisting of superficialities that affect no one's morals, cure no vice, and breed no virtue.[9] In fact, as was so often the case in Hellenistic philosophy, Seneca's primary concern is with ethics.

It is true that Seneca's subject matter is extensive and varied;

yet his attention is ever concentrated upon the question of how men ought to live. He speaks repeatedly of philosophy as devoted to "teaching the art of living" (*Ep.* 95.8; cf. 95.7; 117.12). And he never loses sight of his object; no matter what experience he is describing, the moral is always drawn. This tendency is clearly to be perceived in the *Natural Questions*. Although this work is devoted to a study of nature and cosmology, its aim and *démarche* are ethical, rather than scientific. A number of its most interesting parts are the moral disgressions suggested by the scientific materials. In Book II, for example, lightning recalls to its author other omens, ultimately leading to a discussion of fate and religion. At the close of that book, Seneca concedes that many men would rather be liberated from fear of lightning than comprehend its causes. Averring that every study should possess a moral, Seneca proceeds to argue against the fear of death.

Again, in Book IV, the discussion of snow is displaced at the conclusion of that book by a diatribe against the luxury of Romans who would bathe in snow, or import it to cool their beverages. Throughout his prose writings, Seneca's chief concern is to urge men to grapple with, to come to understand, the meaning of life. His highest, and one may almost say his only, goal is to induce the rescue, the revivification, the progress of souls.

Of course, from the time of the founding father, Zeno, Stoic philosophers of the Porch had endorsed this selfsame goal. After the collapse of Athens at the close of the Hellenic age (404 B.C.), most philosophies had become more esoteric and missionary. From Socrates the Cynics, and subsequently the Stoics as well, had adopted a course which encouraged street-corner harangues and public speeches dealing with ethical questions—how the individual might sustain and come to live with himself in an era of great instability that witnessed the decline of the city-state, public religions, and other institutions.[10] But in Seneca a new note of the *personal* emerges in his endeavor to effect the soul's progress. His *Dialogi* are just that—debates between Seneca and an *adversarius* concerning the *adversarius'* moral plight. Moreover, each dialogue is dedicated directly to the individual. Thus, *De Tranquillitate Animi* is inscribed to Serenus, and Seneca argues with Serenus throughout concerning the latter's restlessness, vacillation, absence of peace of mind. Similarly, the *De Vita Beata* is dedicated to Gallio and argues throughout against reliance upon the crowd

and for achieving that private mental state that will encourage the
happy life. And so with the other moral treatises. Even the traditional "consolations" that Seneca wrote—offering solace to one
who is bereaved—reveal this personal strain, portraying Seneca
struggling with the individual addressed, a Marcia or a Helvia.
There is, simply, throughout much of the prose an intense dramatization of viewpoint that is personal, determined. And the same
qualities are evident in Senecan style—an intense, vibrant, terse
epigrammatic use of language, the renowned *style coupé*.

Such an intense style and particular dramatization of argument
characterize the quality of Seneca's mind, but they also demonstrate the urgency with which he viewed the case for the progress
of the soul. The final goal, of course, is for the individual to arrive
at a state of virtue, to become the *sapiens,* or wise man. But
Seneca distinguishes three classes of *proficientes,* persons traveling along the path of moral progress. First there are those who
are rid of many vices, but not of all. They have eliminated avarice,
for example, but are still subject to anger; they are no longer lust-
ful, but are perhaps haunted by ambition. There is a second class
of those who have suppressed the greatest passions, but who are
not yet secure against a relapse. And there is a third class who
have almost approached wisdom itself. They have dispensed with
passions and vices, but have not yet tested themselves, or put
their wisdom into practice; they lack the final gift of full assurance
reserved for the truly wise (*Ep.* 75.8–14). Through a gradual
progress, therefore, man is to attain the great moral victory of
goodness and wisdom.

Nowhere throughout his writings is Seneca's ardent concern for
the journey to wisdom more in evidence than in the masterwork
of his old age, the *Epistulae Morales,* the 124 moral letters written
to his young friend Lucilius. Here, Seneca has finally found a
form—the short epistle—suitable to the dramatic argumentation
and personal intimacy all his works had, in some way, displayed.
His success in this genre is outstanding, for he virtually gives form
to the modern "essay"—based, appropriately, upon Montaigne's
conception of an *essai,* an attempt or undertaking.[11] In the moral
letters, Seneca is indeed shown conducting the young Lucilius
toward studies, and making his own progress throughout toward
mastering successive stages of the *proficiens.* Specifically, the early
letters are concerned with increasing one's devotion to studies,

and eliminating many a passion and vice (*Ep.* 1–50); the middle period displays one as master of his passions, but subject—as Seneca was—to relapse (*Ep.* 51–90); the last phase urges putting wisdom into practice, testing it, assaying it (*Ep.* 91–123), and the last letter (*Ep.* 124) is concerned with the very doorstep of wisdom, discussing as it does the good as it is to be fully attained by reason.

Much of the basis for Seneca's dramatic and intimate practice derives from his conception of learning by example: it is not enough for one to be harangued with doctrine; man requires models, patterns, examples.[12] These Seneca has provided; his dialogues and epistles present not merely doctrine and dogma but the dramatic examples of mind at work, of mental progress being pursued. Nor is Seneca merely the lofty wise man, directing others; it is crucial that we recognize that he, too, is making the very journey toward wisdom that he solicits in others: "In training another's virtue, one must necessarily train his own" (*Ep.* 109.12). Seneca, like the rest of mankind, is nothing like the final guide; he is only the traveler beside us.

For such a move forward on the path toward perfection, the final guide is the goddess Philosophy. Service to her is perfect freedom (*Ep.* 8.7; 37.3). Philosophy is, ultimately, the mind's health (*Ep.* 15.1–2) and its real joy (*Ep.* 50.9). She arms man against all difficulties; she teaches man to aid the lost, the sick, the needy, and the condemned; she enjoins man to show the ignorant the light of reason (*Ep.* 48.7–9). She alone can arouse us from error (*Ep.* 53.8); she alone embodies the art of living well (*Ep.* 90.1). She is nothing other than life conforming to right reason. Thus, Seneca can urge the identity of philosophy and virtue itself: "There is no philosophy without virtue, nor virtue without philosophy" (*Ep.* 89.8; cf. 90.3). And all progress, in the last analysis, must be directed toward the achievement of wisdom, goodness, virtue, philosophy. "One thing only perfects the soul— the unalterable knowledge of good and evil . . ." (*Ep.* 88.28). To that end, Seneca insisted all his life that every journey should be directed.

II Amicus Humani Generis

"No one is strong enough to emerge from folly by himself; someone must lend him a hand, someone must lead him out,"

Seneca writes in one of his letters (*Ep.* 52.2), and no one can survey the prose writings of Seneca without being struck by his feeling for his fellow men, his sympathy with the human race. As M. L. Clarke observes, "The Stoicism of Seneca marks a break with the intellectualism of earlier Greek thought; it was no longer assumed that to know what was right meant to do what was right. The wise man and the good man were still identified, but there was a shift of emphasis from wisdom to goodness. . . ."[13] Goodness and humanitarianism are among the most significant of Seneca's ideas. They illustrate how far humane thought and sympathy have progressed in philosophy since the time of Aristotle. Abstraction is replaced by particularity; general principles are tempered by views that are more personal.

No one in the Greco-Roman world ever insisted so strongly and repeatedly as did Seneca on man's obligation to live for others, on a commitment to love, mercy, and forgiveness. Again and again he reminds us that no one can live entirely for himself: *Alteri vivas oportet, si vis tibi vivere* ("You must live for another, if you wish to live for yourself," *Ep.* 48.2).[14] Man is born for social communion, which should be exercised by concord, love, and kindness (*Ep.* 95.52),[15] and he who yields to anger, selfishness, or cruelty to his fellow men denies his humanity, degrading himself to the level of the beast (*De Clem.* 1.25.1).

Indeed, Seneca's emphasis upon consideration, love, and tact in the treatment of all men, induces him repeatedly to the condemnation of anger and cruelty.[16] He analyzes anger thoroughly in the three books of his *De Ira*. Discussing the nature of wrath and its causes, he contends that such a passion is unnatural.

Whether anger is in accordance with nature will become clear if we investigate man. What is milder than man in his right mind? What is more cruel than anger? Man is born for mutual aid; anger, for destruction. The one desires harmony, the other, discord. The one to help, the other to harm; the one assists even strangers, the other attacks even the most beloved. . . . Anger, as we have said, is eager to inflict punishment; that such a desire exists in the placid heart of man is not at all in accord with nature. (*De Ira* 1.5.2–3)

Systematically Seneca refutes every argument in defense of rage and passion: "There is nothing great, nothing noble in anger, not even when it appears vehement, scornful of gods and men" (*De*

Ira 1.21.1). Anger's evil effects are stressed. That it is a temporary madness the wise always maintained (*De Ira* 1.1.2); and its lunacy is easily observable by the very appearance of the angry man: his fierce expression, altered color, restless hands, his quick and violent breathing, his gnashing of teeth, his stamping of the foot (*De Ira* 1.1.4). It is similarly noteworthy that children, still barbarous and not yet having attained to reason, are particularly prone to anger—even for frivolous causes (*De Ira* 1.12.4). And, most importantly, Seneca reminds us that ungovernable rage is the one passion that infects whole nations; such lawless and outrageous madness most commonly leads a nation to war (*De Ira* 3.2.2–6).

To check anger, the first necessity is length of time (*De Ira* 2.29.1); reflection will often reveal to one that he has not been injured at all or not so much as he had at first suspected (*De Ira* 3.28.4). Lastly, it is necessary for one to learn what his malady is, to recognize the causes of his anger, in order that he might treat the disease and guard against it (*De Ira* 3.10.4).

Cruelty, a tendency to excessive punishment (*De Clem.* 2.4.1.), is, like anger, directly opposed to the virtue of clemency. In its extremity, it becomes a madness, when the slaying of a man is in itself a pleasure (*De Clem.* 1.25.2). And such madness is progressive: one who relies upon cruelty must protect himself by further acts of cruelty (*De Clem.* 1.13.2). Moreover, Seneca maintains that, ironically enough, bad men are not reformed by harsh punishment, but by milder discipline (*De Clem.* 1.22.1). Indeed, the morals of the whole nation are improved by the sparing administration of punishment (*De Clem.* 1.22.2; 1.23.2; 1.24.1). Thus Seneca again and again stresses the need of remedies for cruelty and chastisement. One remedy is the recollection that we have all erred (*De Clem.* 1.6.3). We should recognize, psychologically, that we constantly display impatience with the faults of others, while condoning or passing over our own (*De Ira* 2.28.8). We are all in some degree weak and defective and consequently men should be tolerant and compassionate of one another.[17] For such reasons, punishments must be inflicted only in extreme cases, and must ever be administered calmly, dispassionately. Chastening is in fact felt more keenly when dispensed by a benevolent man (*De Clem.* 1.22.3). Persistent kindness wins over even bad men (*De Benef.* 7.31.1). Men are capable—and this is signally important—of progress and amendment.

Therefore, the spectacle of greed and ingratitude must not harden us against our fellow men. Let us reflect how many a kindness done to us in early days—the tenderness of a nurse, a friend's advice or relative's aid in times of need—we have carelessly let slip from memory (*De Benef.* 7.28.1–2). The vices which we condemn in others are often found in ourselves. We must forgive others, if we wish to be forgiven. We must overcome evil with good. Setting his standards at the greatest heights, Seneca at one point urges man to imitate the gods themselves, who bestow gifts even upon those who doubt of the existence of deities; and such gods go further, they presevere in giving to the ungrateful (*De Benef.* 7.31.2).

The receiver of my benefaction is ungrateful? He has not wronged me, but himself, for I enjoyed my benefit when I gave it. I shall not for that reason give more tardily, but more carefully. What I lost in the case of this man, I'll gain from others. But even to this man I'll give a benefit again, and like the good farmer, I shall overcome the sterility of the soil by care and cultivation. Failing in this, my benefit may be lost to me, but he is lost to mankind. It is not characteristic of a great soul to confer a benefit and feel its loss. *This* is the great soul—to lose a benefit and to continue giving. (*De Benef.* 7.32)

This daring and noble conception of an *imitatio Dei*—charging men to aspire to godliness—is a recurrent theme in Senecan thought. And such ideas earned him the lasting gratitude of Christianity in later ages and even encouraged his forceful influence on Christian thought.[18] He urges men to "Forgive that you may be forgiven" (*ut absolvaris, ignosce, De Benef.* 7.28.3), or he writes feelingly with an almost Emersonian transcendence and pantheism: *prope est a te deus, tecum est, intus est . . .: sacer intra nos spiritus sedet* ("God is near you, he is with you, he is within you . . .: a sacred spirit resides in us." *Ep.* 41.1–2). At such moments, this philosopher sounds very Christian indeed. But he is a true Stoic, for all of that. The increasing ethical content and spirituality is an inheritance of Middle and Late Stoicism, that is constantly modifying its more coldly formal earlier doctrines into something more personal, humanitarian, and warm. Seneca, more than any other Stoic we know of, is certainly in the vanguard of this reformation. He is a most daring, brazen, neo-Stoic, stipulating firmly that man, through effort, can achieve the status of godhead. No Christian—wary as he was for centuries of *hubris* and that greatest of sins, pride—would go quite so far. And Seneca goes farther: man, unlike the gods, must endure time, nature, and adversity; therefore, when man proves superior to such great trials, he is even superior to God! *Hoc est quo deum antecedatis; ille extra patientiam malorum est, vos supra patientiam.* ("In this one respect you surpass God; he suffers no evil, whereas you transcend it." *De Prov.* 6.6).

Thus, Seneca is never ignorant or forgetful of life's challenges and gloom, nor of the necessity of contending with inevitable adversity;[19] he therefore accentuates benignity and service to his fellow men. Everywhere Seneca recommends generosity and kindliness toward all: "Let us teach man to offer his hand to the shipwrecked, to show the road to the wanderer, to share his bread with the hungry" (*Ep.* 95.51). Man should share his wealth with those in need; he must regard wealth as given him in trust; he is only its steward (*De Benef.* 6.3.2). Charity should be given without hesitation and with pleasure (*De Benef.* 2.1.1). The good man will not refuse a kindness even to a needy enemy (*De Otio.* 1.4), and in giving money to anyone in want he must imply by his manner that he is only paying what the other is entitled to as his fellow man (*De Clem.* 2.6.2; cf. *De Clem.* 1.1.3; *De Vita Beata* 24.3). Man, according to Seneca, is the source and center of our solicitude simply because he is man.

This human appeal in the prose writings is especially characterized by his conception of friendship. He refutes that sordid view of friendship which renders the strength of the tie dependent upon self-interest, as though we desired a friend only to sit by our bedside when we are ill, or to aid us when we are poverty stricken or imprisoned (*Ep.* 9.8). Rather, friendship is the expression of a natural instinct, a need for commitment: "For what reason do I seek a friend? To have someone to die for, someone to follow into exile, someone for whom I would risk my very life" (*Ep.* 9.10). The best philter or love charm to provoke affection in others is to feel such affection oneself (*Ep.* 9.6). Seneca warns that one should consider carefully in choosing a friend, but thereafter give him implicit trust (*Ep.* 3.2). For in the companionship of well-chosen friends there grows up a *sensus communis,* which is an instinctive dedication to sharing and progressing together (see esp. *Ep.* 6).

Related to the bond of friendship is a new and forceful note in

Seneca's writings extolling women. In Greek society, women had virtually no rights; their place was, like the furniture, in the home. Their sensibilities were for the most part ignored, their education scanted.[20] The Roman view had differed little from the Greek. Seneca is concerned in a new way with women; he is concerned with them personally. Two of his three extant *consolationes* are directed to women—to his mother Helvia, and to Marcia, friend of Livia (the mother of Emperor Tiberius). He treats these women with a gentle intimacy, yet he does not fail to urge them, like men, to strive for Stoic discipline and knowledge. He has nothing but praise for his mother and his aunt—their sound training, fine example, and acquired fortitude (*Ad Helv.*, esp. 16.3–4; 19.1–4). Similarly, he speaks most fondly of his wife, Paulina, suggesting that their marriage has evolved into the most worthy friendship, the mating of two souls (*Ep.* 104.2–3).

To be sure, Seneca is very often at pains to condemn what has become an effete, well-to-do, pleasure-loving and debauched society in Rome. Men had always been adulterous, but now most women vie with men in a kind of adulterous competition (*Ep.* 95.20–21). But, as with his treatment of men, Seneca exhorts women to nurture self-control. He will not condone the classic "double standard," which permits husbands to engage in extramarital affairs and yet cautions wives to remain chaste at home (*Ep.* 94.26). Nor is a woman to be honored for a chastity imposed from without or induced by fear (*De Benef.* 4.14.1); she is only chaste when she herself has elected to be so. All of mankind—regardless of sex—must seek an equal knowledge and improvement. Woman, however painted and decorated, is bestial like man— "unless she has acquired learning and much erudition" (*De Cons. Sap.* 14.1). And he does not hesitate to hold up "models" of womanly courage and heroism—Lucretia, Cloelia, and two Cornelias (*Ad Marc.* 16.2–4). But most importantly, he renounces the weary commonplaces that consider women frail vessels and inert pottery: "But who said that nature has dealt spitefully with women's talent and narrowly confined their virtue? Believe me: should they wish it, they have an equal amount of vigor, an equal capacity for the performance of good deeds; they endure grief and suffering equally with men if they have been trained to it" (*Ad Marc.* 16.1).

Of a similar nature is Seneca's attitude toward slavery. It is true that in the period of the early empire a milder attitude toward slaves was developing; many *servi Caesaris* and Roman freedmen came to hold important posts throughout the empire. Nevertheless the recognition of slavery in the ancient world tolerated an institution that was generally cruel, barbarous, inhumane. No other writer was so open and vocal in calling for the amelioration of the slave's condition as Seneca.[21] He openly recognizes the slave's moral rights. He discusses fully the question whether a slave can confer a benefit upon his master; he who denies it, Seneca claims, is ignorant of the rights of man: "For what matters is the benefactor's state of mind, not his social standing. Virtue excludes no one; she opens her doors to all, she admits all, summons all—the freeborn and the emancipated, slaves, kings, and exiles; she does not regard residence or property, she is satisfied with man unadorned" (*De Benef.* 3.18.2).

He earnestly repudiates the idea that a slave's service, however excellent, is merely a "duty" owed to his master, a duty which, as it springs from constraint, is undeserving of gratitude (*De Benef.* 3.19.1). By such a principle, a subject cannot confer a benefit on his king, a soldier on his general (*De Benef.* 3.18.3). There is, on the contrary, Seneca affirms, a limit beyond which power cannot command obedience. One must surely distingiush between cringing compliance and noble self-sacrifice. Slaves have often endured injury and even death to save their master's life in battle. They have often suffered the last extremity of torture rather than betray their master's secrets (*De Benef.* 3.21.1–2; 3.19.3; 3.25).

Only the body of a slave belongs to his lord, his mind belongs to himself and is free (*De Benef.* 3.20.1). He is as capable of virtue and of culture as all other men. The condition in which a man is born, Seneca warns, is not to be confused with the man himself. After describing the good and upright soul as a god dwelling in man's body, he insists that "This soul can inhabit a Roman knight or a freedman or a slave. For what is a Roman knight or freedman or slave? Names born of ambition or injustice" (*Ep.* 31.11).

In *Epistle* 47 to Lucilius he discusses the treatment of slaves, in what is his most famous passage on the subject. Contemptuously, he details the haughty inhumanity of many a wealthy master surrounded by a multitude of cowering menials in whom he saw, according to the Roman proverb, "as many enemies as slaves" (*Ep.* 47.5). The proverb is false, Seneca declares. It is the master's fault if he has transformed his slaves into foes. They will certainly be his friends if he treats them with kindness and associates with them on easy terms, remembering that they, too, are men of flesh and blood, like himself. In a speech that almost recalls Portia's celebration of mercy in Shakespeare's *Merchant of Venice*, Seneca refutes his *adversarius:*

"They are slaves" [claims the adversary]. On the contrary, men. "They are slaves." On the contrary, comrades. "They are slaves." On the contrary, modest friends. "They are slaves." On the contrary, fellow-slaves, if you reflect that fortune has equal power over all. . . . Remember, that he whom you call your slave sprang from the same seed, enjoys the same sky, lives, breathes, and dies in the same way as you yourself . . . ! Live with your slave benignly, affably, and admit him into your conversation, into your counsels, into your feasts. . . . Let some dine with you because they are worthy; others, that they may become so. . . . There is no reason, my Lucilius, why you should seek a friend only in the Forum or in the Senate; if you pay careful attention, you'll even find one at home. . . . Just as he is a fool who, when buying a horse, does not inspect the horse itself, but merely the saddle and bridle, so is he most foolish who judges a man by his clothing or his position, mere robes and equipment that cover us. (*Ep.* 47.1, 10, 13, 15, 16)

This regular concern for the soul within all men and for the potential friendship among men leads Seneca to denounce boldly and candidly the slaughter taking place at the popular gladiatorial shows. He simply condemns the brutality with which criminals were exposed to wild beasts at the "entertainments" while the audience looked on and cheered at the barbarous sport. He protests to his friend Lucilius against the demoralizing influence such scenes must have upon man's character and temperament: " 'But so-and-so committed highway robbery; he killed a man' [someone might object]. Well, then, because he killed, he deserved such a public execution.—But what crime have you committed, poor fool, that compels you to watch it?" (*Ep.* 7.5). From attending such games, from lingering with the crowd, he observes, paradoxically but understandably, one becomes less human (*Ep.* 7.2–3). As a consequence, he frequently condemns all such chilling amusements in an age that honored them.[22] He sustains, instead, the lofty principle that man must be an object of reverence in the eyes of man: *Homo sacra res homini.* Man must not be massacred in jest and sport (*Ep.* 95.33).

For similar reasons Seneca absolutely condemns warfare. He asks why we seek to restrain manslaughter and individual murders when we honor the crime of butchering whole peoples (*Ep.* 95.30; *N.Q.* 5.18.5, 7–12). Should crimes receive a different designation because they have been committed by generals in uniform? Is not man, the supposedly most benign class of beings, ashamed to take pleasure in beholding the slaughter of his fellow men? (*Ep.* 95.31). In an era that celebrated military action, Seneca called carnage into question.

And there was good reason why Seneca opposed chauvinistic competition and international strife. As a Stoic, Seneca frequently propounds the thesis that every man is born into two communities —into his local and native city, the Athens or Carthage to which he is committed by the accident of birth, but also into the great universal society of gods and men, wide as the courses of the sun, the Cosmopolis.[23] The wise man will esteem this larger community, to which all men belong, far above any particular city in which he resides (*De Tranq. An.* 4.4). Amid this great citizenry of the world all distinctions of race, nationality, and class are to be subordinated to a sense of kinship and brotherhood. If human society is based upon that unique quality common to individuals —reason (*Ep.* 76.9–10)—we have no right to limit this society to a single nation, or to believe ourselves more nearly related to some men than to others. All men, apart from what they have made themselves by their own efforts, are equally kindred, since all equally share the quality of reason. The same nature has fashioned all men from the same elements for the same destiny (*Ep.* 95.52); therefore we are all, bond or free, ruler or subject, citizens of the universal commonwealth. All human beings are capable of progressing along the same route and of attaining to virtue (*Ep.* 108.8). And as such, all men are natural-born citizens of the Cosmopolis.

We should realize, consequently, that Seneca's is both a leveling and a lofty creed. It recognizes only one claim to rank or nobility—the capacity for and the attainment of virtue (*De Benef.* 3.28.1; *Ep.* 44.4–5). It embraces in the universal commonwealth all human souls, freeborn or slave, male or female, emperor or peasant, heedless of how they might be classed by accident or fortune. Seneca devoted his energies and expended his life in an effort to shape that earthly commonwealth and to foster membership in it. He always honored love and kindness, compassion and forbearance throughout his private—and his public—career. So often well in advance of his time in his principles and convictions, this *amicus humani generis* championed significant human values with outspokenness, virility, and zeal. His philosophic precepts and memorable sentiments reveal genuine feeling and profound understanding of mankind and its aspirations.

III *Divinity: Nature, Fate, and Reason*

If Seneca is powerfully committed to philanthropy, the aiding of his fellow men, he is likewise committed to philotheism, the adoration of God. Frequently in his writings, it is God's cause that Seneca claims to plead.[24] He holds this deity to be the supreme ruler of the universe,[25] the creator of this universe,[26] himself the best part of his own creation (*N.Q.* 7.30.3–4), the greatest and most powerful force in the universe (*Ep.* 31.10; 58.17). Seneca urges that the vast and marvelous structure of the universe cannot endure without a supreme ruler to guide and preserve it (*De Prov.* 1.2). Moreover, he argues, human nature is so constituted as to discover these truths (*Ep.* 117.6). For a little thought on the part of any man will reveal to him that there must be a power inherent in the universe that moves and directs its operations, just as the soul is the body's prime mover (*Ep.* 65.24).

Together with the Stoics, Seneca believed that this supreme power is one God appearing under many names, it mattering little what he be termed. In the *Ad Helviam*, Seneca writes: "whoever the creator of the universe was—whether an omnipotent God, or incorporeal Reason, shaper of enormous works, or a divine spirit equally permeating all things, the largest and the smallest, or Fate and an immutable chain of causes adhering one to another . . ." (*Ad Helv.* 8.3).[27] Thus, God is not, for Seneca and the Stoics, anything like the traditional Judaeo-Christian conception of deity. He is a divine and coherent principle rather than an anthropomorphic figure of mystery and wrath. Indeed, Seneca frequently speaks of nature, fate, and reason as being identical with God;[28] the terms are all analogous. Such a God is the great spirit in the universe, the exemplar of reality itself, however he may be described by human speech. He is that impalpable, primary, and creative force which inhabits all the phenomena of physical nature and all the species of human life (*De Benef.* 4.72). For Seneca and the Stoics, all things proceed from God, and to him they all will return at last, when each cycle of time has run its course, the old emanations are absorbed into the source of life, and the formation of a new world begins afresh.[29] "Whatever exists will cease to exist; it will not, however, perish, but will be dissolved . . .; [the mind] would endure more bravely its own end and the loss of all that belongs to it, if it could only hope that life and death, like all else, alternate, that whatever has been composed is decomposed and whatever has been decomposed is composed, and that the eternal, artful God, who controls all things, turns his attention to this task" (*Ep.* 71.14). Seneca is, like all the Stoics, a pantheist. He believes that the world is identified with deity—the efficient cause of the universe, described by different names, which pervades the vast mass of inert matter.[30] Seneca would certainly agree, for instance, with the vision of Wordsworth, who, in contemplating nature, was struck by

> . . . a sense sublime
> Of something far more deeply interfused,
> Whose dwelling is the light of setting suns,
> And the round ocean and the living air,
> And the blue sky, and in the mind of man;
> A motion and a spirit, that impels
> All thinking things, all objects of all thought,
> And rolls through all things.[31]

Matter and spirit are not, as they were for Aristotle, entities altogether different though eternally united. On the contrary, creative spirit is inerfused in rude matter; it is itself something material, and is considered identical with Reason, or Breath, or the primary element Fire.[32] This is the pervasive Stoic conception of a harmonious monism, as distinct from the dualism of Plato. Such a deity is an imminent seed or power that dwells within all things, a flame that sparks their growth and development. God is simultaneously, therefore, the primary matter as well as the principle force that shapes derivative materials of which all things are made.[33] He is the ubiquitous force, the rational principle that penetrates everything, is present everywhere. He is obviously dedicated to coherent principles and laws of development and is thereby identified with Fate and Nature itself.

Moreover, such a philosophy as this endorses a pantheism of the internal spirit—every soul is of divine origin, a part of the divine fire, an emanation and representation of God himself (*Ad Helv.* 6.7; *Ep.* 92.30). Thus, all men possess a rational nature common in its origin with the very reason (or *logos*) that creates and rules the cosmos (*Ep.* 66.12).[34] "God is near you, he is with you, he is within you. A sacred spirit resides in us, one who observes our good and bad acts and is our guardian" (*Ep.* 41.1–2).

Just as God is the force inherent in all nature making for unity, so he is the secret power within man making for virtue. "Do you wonder that man goes to the gods? God comes to men; rather, what is closer, he comes into men; there is no good mind without God" (*Ep.* 73.16). In another *Epistle*, Seneca calls the upright, good, and great soul a God dwelling in a human body (*Ep.* 31.11).

Hence God is a spiritual and moral being, the source and encouragement of righteousness, the divine seed within us. He is the witness of our deeds, omnipresent, omniscient, and invisible (*Ep.* 10.5; 83.1). He is our protector and our guide, and his spirit resides in our hearts. Consequently—and this is an important point —man has no need for prayer and worship. God, Seneca maintains, dwells not in temples of wood or stone but in the human heart (*Ep.* 31.5; 41.1; 115.5). Seneca is outspoken in deriding vain superstition,[35] claiming that God certainly takes no delight in ritual sacrifices that shed the blood of victims (*De Benef.* 1.6.3). Nor does God yearn for the ministrations of human servants. Far from it, he himself, rather, serves mankind; everywhere and to all men, he is at hand to give aid (*Ep.* 95.47).[36]

And our duty to God or to the gods is simple indeed; we are to believe in them, to acknowledge their greatness and benevolence, and to recognize them as the creators and rulers of the universe (*Ep.* 95.50). We need not light lamps in their honor on Sabbath days nor throng in their temples to offer morning salutations: we need not bring Jove a towel or Juno a mirror (*Ep.* 95.47). Our service to them is to follow and to imitate them; he who wishes to win their favor must be a good man: "Do you wish to obtain the favor of the gods? Be a good man. He who has imitated them has worshipped them enough" (*Ep.* 95.50).

It is true, of course, that the imitation of God, the imitation of

Nature has as a principle been criticized for its abstractness and opacity. Thus, in a famous passage from *Rasselas,* when the Prince asks a philosopher to clarify what he means by "living according to nature," the philosopher placidly answers: " 'To live according to nature' is to act always with due regard to the fitness arising from the relations and qualities of causes and effects; to concur with the great and unchangeable scheme of universal felicity; to cooperate with the general disposition and tendency of the present system of things."[37]

The obscure language of this passage is amusing, and poor Rasselas is sent away no wiser than when he had come. But Seneca is not guilty of generating such a verbose befuddlement. Neither does he ever suggest the "ease" with which one might follow Nature or God, nor imply that the world offers "universal felicity." Seneca does point up the analogy between man's reason as governing the body and God's *ratio* as governing the universe (*Ep.* 65.24; 92.32); yet he clearly recognizes that, whereas God's reason is perfect and eternal, man's reason is merely potential. Thus, children are without reason (*Ep.* 121.14; 124.9; *De Benef.* 3.31.2), and man can only slowly apply reason to taming the violence of his fears and the madness of his desires (*Ep.* 82.6; *N.Q.* 6.2.1). The secrets of the gods are revealed only gradually to men (*N.Q.* 7.30.3–6). Progress toward the life of reason was always viewed as a real possibility for man (*Ep.* 90.1–2); with the seed of virtue within him, man is capable of being aided by guidance and advice from others, and capable of helping himself.[38] "Nature does not give virtue; to become good is an art" (*Ep.* 90.44). Men proceed by degrees on the path of progress. But there is no facile optimism in Seneca's view; he concedes that the ideal wise man is indeed a rarity—occurring as often as the phoenix, once in every five hundred years.[39] Yet this discernment does not prevent Seneca from urging that man continually strive to perfect himself, that he constantly endeavor to imitate God's benevolence and wisdom. Again and again Seneca reminds us that only through one's own personal effort can he become more virtuous, more like God.

Nor must the man on the path of moral progress lose hope when his fortune seems adverse. In one of his paradoxes Seneca observes that the gods "punish" the unworthy—by bestowing upon them seeming goods! (*Ep.* 95.50; 110.2). And the reverse of this is also true: the gods "reward" the good man by bestowing upon him seeming evils. "How often, to be sure, has so-called calamity been the source and beginning of happiness!" (*Ep.* 110.3). The whole of the *De Providentia* is thus concerned with demonstrating that the gods only *seem* to punish the good man; that adversity is the great test and reward of the heroic and the good man. Everywhere in his prose Seneca renounces the easy road or the soft cushion; he views the man who regardless of fortune would face adversity and compete with gods as truly noble: "What wonder that those attempting a steep path do not reach the top? But if you are a man, look up to those striving for great things, even though they fall" (*De Vita Beata* 20.2). Thus, the struggling man (the *proficiens*) approaches the heroic nature of the gods themselves; and the wise man (the *sapiens*) is similar to God in all things save his mortality.[40] Having fought the good fight, having attained wisdom, and having conquered his fear of mortality, he is indeed superior to God (*Ep.* 53.11; 73.14; *De Prov.* 6.6).

As a consequence, the true worship of God is never achieved by formal prayer or ritual sacrifice; it consists in man's striving to know and to imitate God's infinite goodness and knowledge. Only through his own endeavors and contention can he become more virtuous. By fostering the divine seeds within him, man *can* bring his reason to perfection, and, daringly, become God's equal. Seneca advocates, then, but one single form of worship, the study of philosophy, which teaches virtue. To him, philosophy is the sole guide in life. He can conceive of no loftier precepts, no nobler teachings, than those which philosophy proffers mankind: "For this is what philosophy promises me, that she will make me equal to God" (*Ep.* 48.11).

IV   Meditatio Mortis

Seneca's reference to man's endeavor to become "equal to the gods" (*Ep.* 48.11) is, in his philosophy, a recurrent theme. The *sapiens*, he asserts, has achieved an element of godliness (*Ep.* 87.19) and, save for his mortality, is similar to God in all things.[41] He even compares the *sapiens* overtly to Jupiter (*Ep.* 9.16; 73.12–15). Indeed, as mentioned above, the wise man in a manner excels God (*Ep.* 53.11; 73.14; *De Prov.* 6.6). Even the *proficiens*, the potentially good man, is portrayed as ever aspiring, ever striving toward the goal that is virtually divine.[42] "A man is truly noble when he, regarding not his physical strength, but his strength of character, diligently strives, attempts lofty goals and conceives in his thought greater projects than those which can be accomplished even by men endowed with great minds" (*De Vita Beata* 20.2). Such an aspirant says to himself, "I shall endure labors, however great they will be, sustaining my body by my soul" (*De Vita Beata* 20.2–3). The emphasis here upon endeavor, upon "labor," reminds us that it was just such qualities of strength and willingness to labor that had made, first, the Cynics and, then the Stoics select Hercules as their archetypal pattern. And Hercules, of course, had ultimately achieved deification—that sacred goal at journey's end.

Because the would-be *sapiens* is ever attempting, with Herculean effort to rise upward to Deity, it is only fitting that we inquire what Seneca's attitude was toward the afterlife. We should want to know his opinion concerning immortality, the possibility of man's finally rising, after death, to dwell among the very gods whom he has, throughout his lifetime, so striven to approach.[43]

If, as Seneca claimed, a spirit dwells within us, it would seem only fitting that, after death, we should dwell in spirit. In his *consolationes* particularly Seneca does accentuate such a view. Thus, he consoles Marcia for the loss of her son: "Only the image of your son and a likeness unlike him has perished; he himself is indeed eternal and enjoys now a far better state, relieved of external burdens and left entirely to himself" (*Ad Marc.* 24.5). Previously, the boy's soul had been a prisoner of the flesh. "The soul ever struggles with the burden of the flesh so as not to be dragged down and sunk; it strives to ascend to that place from which it descended. There, eternal rest awaits it, beholding purity and brightness, having withdrawn from confusion and darkness" (*Ad Marc.* 24.5). But now, "He is complete, and, leaving nothing of himself on earth, he has fled and wholly departed; he loitered for a little while above us, while he was being cleansed and purged of his vices and of every mortal blemish; then, lifted on high, he sped to the souls of the blessed" (*Ad Marc.* 25.1).[44] With imagery echoing Plato's "myth of the cave,"[45] he describes the soul as yearning for the light. "Then our soul will have reason to rejoice when released from this darkness in which it is tumbled; it will not have perceived the brightness dimly but will have encountered broad daylight and will have returned to its own place in the sky . . ." (*Ep.* 79.12). After the manner of Scipio's dream,[46] the soul will rise above the lower atmosphere and observe all of heaven's light shining with equal radiance: "At some time the secrets of nature will be revealed to you, that mist will be driven away, and clear light will penetrate on every side" (*Ep.* 102.28).

We should observe, however, that his imagery of the soul's (the breath's) rising to its proper sphere, to the light, is extremely generalized; the suggestions of scenes from Plato and Cicero render this vision traditional. Furthermore, as Seneca more than once observes, this spiritual transcendence is a common, that is, a popular, expectation: "When we discuss the immortality of the soul, the consensus of mankind, either fearing or worshipping spirits below, has considerable weight with us" (*Ep.* 117.6). Such a popular tale is even likely to be the fond wish of better men: "If only the report of wise men is true and some region receives us, then perhaps he who we think has perished has been sent on ahead" (*Ep.* 63.16). The note of doubt in such passages is distinct and clear: "if only the soul continues to exist when freed from the body, a happier condition awaits it . . ." (*Ep.* 76.25).

Elsewhere, in one of his highest flights of solace, comforting Polybius on the loss of his brother, Seneca again displays some reservation. Your brother is free at last, he writes. "Now he enjoys the open and free heavens; from a humble and lowly position he has risen to that place, *whatever that place may be* (*quisquis ille est*), which receives in its blessed embrace souls freed from bondage, and now he freely wanders there and with highest pleasure clearly perceives all of nature's blessings" (*Ad Polyb.* 9.8). [Italics mine.] Nor is there merely a *quisquis ille est* appended to a number of his statements about the afterlife; there is a distinct tendency to regard such a visionary scheme as merely a "dream." He opens one epistle to Lucilius by claiming that he had been pursuing a pleasant "dream": "It delighted me to consider the immortality of the soul, even, by Hercules, to believe in it. For I easily gave myself over to the opinion of great men who promise rather than prove this most pleasant state. I surrendered myself to such a great hope" (*Ep.* 102.2). Then he jocularly adds that the arrival of Lucilius' latest letter has abruptly roused him, making him "lose that pretty dream." Such a dream, he explained at the outset, was *falsum.*

To Seneca, it appears equally likely that after death there is nothingness. "Nothing can injure him who does not exist" (*Ep.* 99.30). "Death is non-existence . . ." (*Ep.* 54.4). "It's all the same: you will not be, you were not" (*Ep.* 77.11). Upon several occasions, it is true, Seneca almost seems to endorse metempsychosis —the reappearance of one's spirit in another body.

> But if you have so great a desire for a longer life, reflect that none of those things are destroyed which disappear from sight and are reassimilated into nature (*in rerum naturam*) from which they issued and are soon to issue again; these objects cease their existence but do not perish. And death, which we fear and reject, interrupts life, it does not snatch it away; the time will come again which will restore us to the light of day, which many would be unwilling to accept, if it did not bring them back forgetful of the past. (*Ep.* 36.10)

This discussion of an eternal recurrence *in rerum naturam* is reminiscent of Lucretius, and it is quite likely that Seneca, like the Epicurean poet, alludes merely to the chance reassemblage of the particles of man in the distant future. Thus, even such a possible recurrence may be used as but one further argument against the fear of death; this is precisely Lucretius' argument:

> So, when our mortal frame shall be disjoyn'd,
> The lifeless Lump, uncoupled from the mind,
> From sense of grief and pain we shall be free;
> We shall not feel, because we shall not *Be*.
> Though Earth in Seas, and Seas in Heav'n were lost,
> We should not move, we only shou'd be tost.
> Nay, ev'n suppose when we have suffer'd Fate,
> The Soul cou'd feel in her divided state,
> What's that to us? for we are only we
> While Souls and bodies in one frame agree.
> Nay, tho' our Atoms shou'd revolve by chance,
> And matter leape into the former dance;
> Tho' time our Life and motion cou'd restore,
> And make our Bodies what they were before,
> What gain to us wou'd all this bustle bring?
> The new made man wou'd be another thing;
> When once an interrupting pause is made,
> That individual Being is decay'd.
> We, who are dead and gone, shall bear no part

> In all the pleasures, nor shall feel the smart,
> Whom of our Matter Time shall mould anew.
> . . . .
> And since the Man who *Is* not, feels not woe,
> (For death exempts him, and wards off the blow,
> Which we, the living, only feel and bear)
> What is there left for us in death to fear?
> When once that pause of life has come between
> 'Tis just the same as we had never been.[47]

The reconstitution of soul and body, like the regrouping of so many atoms, will produce a different personality, another self; the present self in effect simply ceases to be.

Moreover, such a suggestion of eternal return should remind us that Seneca, like most Stoics, at least formally (however slightly) accepts the theory of the universe's cyclic creation and destruction; periodically, the world is consumed by fire, and commences anew. By this hypothesis, even the soul surviving death will in the fullness of time be destroyed, although a new creation follows.[48]

> And when the time shall come in which the world will be destroyed in order to be born again, all things will be annihilated of themselves and stars will collide with stars and whatever now shines in orderly arrangement will blaze together, all things burning in the conflagration. At that time, we souls of the blessed, who have been allotted immortality, when it shall seem best to God to inflict again this destruction, while the universe is collapsing, shall be a small addition to an immense ruin and shall be changed into our former elements. (*Ad Marc.* 26.6)[49]

In the *Apology,* Socrates had explained that death was one of two things, either annihilation or the transformation and removal of the soul to Hades, and that both of these were "good."[50] Like Socrates, Seneca is equivocal on this subject and unwilling to take an absolute stand. He normally refuses to declare on either side, whether the soul shall eternally live, or whether the soul shall surely die. Most of his statements about death include *both* possibilities: "What is death? Either the end or a transformation" (*Ep.* 65.24). "Death either destroys the soul or removes it from the body" (*Ep.* 24.18). "Let the great soul obey God and endure without hesitation whatever the law of the universe orders; for either the great soul is sent forth to a better life to dwell in brighter light and deeper calm among things divine or at any rate without any inconvenience to itself, it will be recompounded and return to the universe" (*Ep.* 71.16).

It is important, here, to recognize that, for Seneca, the problem was not one of confusion or doubt, but a relevant topic to be considered and contemplated *in this life*. As J. N. Sevenster has observed, Seneca was, for instance, certain to draw an object "lesson from Canus who, when condemned to death by Caligula, continued to search for truth until the very end 'and to make his own death a subject for debate,' *ex morte sua quaestionem habere*. In my belief Seneca . . . considered death as a *quaestio*. Nothing can be said about it with certainty. But whatever the outcome may be, whether there is a life after death or not, death is not a cause for grief."[51] And it is precisely such *innumerabiles quaestiones* that Seneca accentuates:

One must learn about things divine and human, about the past and future, about the perishable and the everlasting, about time. . . . Concerning the soul itself there are innumerable questions. . . .

Whatever portion of things human and divine you have comprehended, you will be exhausted by the great quantity of things that must be questioned and learned. In order that these topics, so many and so weighty, can have lodging in the mind, superfluous items must be removed. Virtue will not submit to narrow bounds; a great subject requires extensive space. Let all else be expelled; let the whole heart lie open to virtue. (*Ep.* 88.33–35)

What is emphasized in this passage is study of matters of central importance in the creation, study in the course of one's lifetime. As an ethical philosopher, Seneca's concern is with *this life*—how it is lived. He would thoroughly agree with Samuel Johnson, who, seventeen hundred years later, is still voicing the central dicta of Socratic tradition: "It was [Socrates'] labour to turn philosophy from the study of nature to speculations upon life; but the innovators whom I oppose are turning off attention from life to nature. They seem to think that we are placed here to watch the growth of plants, or the motions of the stars. Socrates was rather of opinion, that what we had to learn was, how to do good, and avoid evil. . . . The first requisite is the religious and moral knowledge of right and wrong."[52] The renowned Stoic slave philosopher Epictetus, just a little after Seneca's time, makes this same point: "What do I care whether all things are composed of atoms or other particles, or of fire and earth? Isn't it enough to learn the true nature of good and evil. . . ?"[53] Seneca's emphasis is precisely the same: "The soul is perfected by one thing only—the immutable knowledge of good and evil" (Ep. 88.28). Accordingly, Seneca stressed ethical conduct here and now; the good life and study toward becoming virtuous. toward living—and dying—well are his chief concerns. Therefore, not death and the afterlife are to him of primary importance, but conduct in life, and the preparation for death. And we discover that with him *meditatio mortis* is a predominant theme. He writes to Lucilius, "meanwhile Epicurus will be appropriate, who says: 'Meditate upon death,' or, if it is more suitable, this meaning may be conveyed to us thus: 'It is a noble thing to learn how to die'" (Ep. 26.8–9). It is important enough for Seneca to repeat the words again in the same epistle, *Meditare mortem.* And it is confirmed elsewhere: "If you will listen to me, meditate and practice this: how you may welcome death, or even, should circumstances require, summon it" (*Ep.* 69.6). The very climax of the *De Ira* urges one to restrain his wrath by *cogitatio mortalitatis*: "You have no time to lose!" (*De Ira* 3.42.2). That time cannot be wasted is a repeated motif in Seneca, for one needs every available moment to achieve even slight mastery of one's self and one's life. "Scarcely will an entire lifetime suffice to subdue and restrain vices swollen by long-continued licence, not to mention reducing so brief a time by interruptions" (*Ep.* 69.5–6). In addition, Seneca clearly recognizes that it not only requires a whole lifetime to learn how to live—but a whole lifetime to learn how to die (*De Brev. Vit.* 7.3). Over and over again Seneca insists that death is the one subject man could never meditate upon in vain. Therefore, training one's self for the incontestable event is imperative. Since, obviously, one's dying is his final gesture, the last visible sign of his lifetime, it is evident that the manner of one's death displays the real strength of a man's soul (*Ep.* 26.5–6).

Preparation for death is singularly present in Seneca's own mind and repeatedly calls forth from him a heated and powerful response: "Death pursues me, life escapes me; teach me something that will help!" (*Ep.* 49.9). "I have confronted every day as if it were my last" (*Ep.* 93.6). Patently, this acute awareness of death on Seneca's part—and it is a topic he raises with striking persistence—has a strong foundation in the very nature of his personality. For one thing, Seneca himself had always suffered from ill health. He had been tormented and aggrieved at length from many a disease,[54] and was an aging man, in his late sixties, when he composed the *Epistulae Morales*. Indeed, illness had caused him, even at an early age, seriously to contemplate suicide (*Ep.* 78.2). Furthermore, as a man having lived during the reigns of Tiberius, Caligula, Claudius, and Nero, he was a repeated witness to court intrigue, murder, and assassination. Anyone perusing the pages of Tacitus' *Annals* will be struck by the relentless parade of machinations and slaughter that bedeck and bedaub this period. If Seneca speaks frequently of living each day as if it were his last, he is simply being realistic and prudent. Intellectuals and aristocrats could anticipate a life expectancy of short duration.

As a consequence of all these factors, Seneca speaks often and at length in his writings of suicide.[55] Suicide had become, in the empire, particularly among the wealthy, the persecuted, and the dissolute, a fashionable mode of exodus. For such a popular custom, to be sure, Seneca has contempt, and he rebukes those who merely lust after death for its own sake (*Ep.* 24.25), or who would commit suicide because they suffered from curable illnesses, experienced a fear of death, or encountered boredom and weariness with life.[56] Nor will he endorse that selfish suicide which permits one to escape responsibilities to family and friends.[57]

On the other hand, when circumstances over which one has no control render continuance in life no longer desirable, Seneca, like many an influential Stoic before him,[58] advocates self-destruction. Severe infirmity in old age, madness or the crippling of one's mental powers, any incurable disease, drastic poverty, and the tyranny of a despot that is inescapable—all these comprise justifiable reasons for taking one's life.[59] Suicide is essential among Seneca's moral doctrines; it assures that complete freedom of the human psyche which his philosophy so much certified and endorsed. "He who denies the right of committing suicide," Seneca affirms, "obstructs the road to liberty." "Eternal law did nothing better than when it provided us with one entry way to life but many exits" (*Ep.* 70.14). If man is too much subject in life to chance, fate, the necessities of nature and of empire, he is at least free in the governing of his mind, his responses, his actions—and the length of his life. As Albert Salomon has asserted, Stoicism insisted upon "making the subjective consciousness the foundation of philosophy. . . . [Stoic] Philosophy as a way of life makes men free. It is the last stand of liberty in a world of servitude."[60]

Thus, to Seneca's mind, suicide becomes an essential ethical consideration because it assures one of that complete freedom of mind which his philosophy so much extolled. The mark of the wise man's independence of external coercions and events is precisely a man's being able to quit life at his pleasure (*Ep.* 65.22; 70.4). Consequently, for Seneca, the self-murder of Cato of Utica represents a laudable example; it is the crowning instance of a wise man's triumph over destiny and is exemplary of the victory of the human will.[61] Suicide, thus viewed, is the culminating expression of moral freedom.

This decided attention to death and suicide surely indicates that these topics struck a special personal as well as philosophic chord in Seneca, eliciting from him some of his longest and most profound meditations. But it does not follow, therefore, that Seneca was in some pathological sense "obsessed" with death.[62] On the contrary, Seneca lived to a ripe old age and did *not* take his own life until commanded to do so by his emperor and executioner. Rather, it ought to be perceived that Seneca's philosophic devotion was to life itself, and how it was to be lived. His pages are filled wtih commentary about living well and with honor. The duty and proof of life, he contends, consist in one's action (*Ep.* 122.3); and it is within the reach of every man to live nobly (*Ep.* 22.17; 93.7). Nothing, he concedes, is more difficult to learn than the art of living (*De Brev. Vit.* 7.3–4), but living well can be learned—from philosophy (*Ep.* 90.1). Again and again he reiterates that it is not life's length that is important but the quality of that life.[63]

Death, therefore, must be set in its proper perspective. It is the inevitable rounding off of one's life. As a result, it becomes the apex of one's life, the fifth act of the play; and the manner of one's dying reveals, once and for all, the nature of one's soul (*Ep.* 26.5–6). One must equally pursue the life of greatest honor (*Ep.* 104.23) and a most honorable death (*Ep.* 77.6). The two are interfused. Thus the wise man must depart courageously, whether he depart to a heaven or to the void, because it is the last act of one's living. Honor and courage are pursued for themselves; the wise man's emphasis is upon the nature of his soul *in life*. For this reason, the *sapiens* does not conjecture about the afterlife, he concentrates upon himself and what he *is*. "Nor, says the wise man, do I depart more bravely because of the hope arising from my judgment that a path lies open to me to the gods. I have, to be sure, deserved being admitted to their company, and have already been among them and have sent my soul to them as they have sent theirs to me. But suppose I am excluded, and that after death nothing of man remains; my courage is equally great, even if I depart on a journey—to nowhere" (*Ep.* 93.10).

Seneca was not alone in this emphasis upon the whole of one's life, including its finale. When the great Theban commander Epaminondas (5th century B.C.) had been asked who deserved the most esteem—Chabrias, Iphicrates, or himself—he replied that it was difficult to determine while the three of them were still alive.[64] In the same fashion, when the enormously wealthy Lydian King, Croesus (6th century B.C.), wished to obtain respect for his life because of his wealth and prosperity, Solon replied that we must "regard the end" of every matter and that one cannot judge a man's life until he has ended it well.[65]

So it was with Seneca himself. If we assess the whole pattern of his life and "regard his end," then we can understand him. By his own courageous death, he, too, like Cato and Socrates, became the pattern and the exemplar. In his own dying, he lived up to his prescriptive standards with a brilliant success, for "when the moment came for Seneca to test his own training for death, his philosophy of life found in him an authentic illustration."[66] He met death, as he had so long striven to live, with honor.

V   *Eclecticism*

Not only are we struck by Seneca's noble and courageous death but by the whole pattern of his life, which can best be described as "eclectic." Although he allied himself to the Stoics more closely than to any other group of philosophers, yet he continually nurtured his intellectual development from innumerable sources, authors, and philosophic schools. "We may say that those perform genuine service who desire to establish a daily intimacy with Zeno, Pythagoras, Democritus, Aristotle, and Theophrastus, and all the other masters of meaningful knowledge . . ." (*De Brev. Vit.* 14.5). "I venerate them and rise when such great masters are mentioned" (*Ep.* 64.10).

It is true, to be sure, that by the time of the Middle Stoa in the

78   SENECA

first century B.C., Stoic leaders like Panaetius and Posidonius had
themselves become "eclectic." Indeed, it was a general trend observable in all the schools. Academics, Cynics, Peripatetics, Cyre-
naics, and the like had ceased what had been for several centuries
a brawling over the finer distinctions of doctrine. All the schools
had increasingly come to emphasize, not a broad range of studies
—in physics, metaphysics, psychology, esthetics—but a singular
concern for ethics, for moral conduct. "And in the purely moral
sphere to which philosophy was now confined, the natural tendency of the different schools, not even excluding the Epicurean,
was to assimilation and electicism."[67] "From these circumstances
there emerged the type which we now call the 'eclectic,' but
which the Romans called simply the 'philosopher'; that is, the
man who drew practical wisdom from all sources alike, binding
himself to the dogmas of no school, but winning his way by apt-
ness of discourse and sympathy of manner to social importance."[68]

Seneca is certainly not exempt from this climate replete with
traveling and teaching "philosophers." As a youth he had come
under the influence of a number of philosophers from the various
schools. He studied with Sotion, the Pythagorean philosopher
whose zeal even persuaded Seneca, for a time, to become a vege-
tarian (*Ep.* 49.2; 108.17–22). He speaks fondly of the Stoic philosopher Attalus, at whose school Seneca was the first to arrive each
day (*Ep.* 108.2–3, 13–16, 23). Similarly, he had early attended the
lectures of Fabianus Papirius, of the Sextian school (*Ep.* 100.12;
cf. 11.4; 52.11). And the Cynic philosopher Demetrius, who had
been a powerful speaker, was ever held by Seneca in highest
esteem (*Ep.* 62.3; *De Benef.* 7.1.3; 7.8.2).

Such a varied education is well reflected in Seneca's own inclusive philosophy: "I am free to dispute with Socrates, doubt with
Carneades, achieve tranquillity with Epicurus, conquer human
nature with the Stoics, exceed it with the Cynics" (*De Brev. Vit.*
14.2). For Seneca feels that the mere slavish addiction to a single
school is a kind of fanaticism: "when someone always adheres to
one man's opinion, he is not in the Senate but in a faction" (*De
Otio* 3.1). Elsewhere he insists that independent thinking is especially necessary for a man who follows his own course, being
enslaved to none of his predecessors (*Ep.* 80.1).

As a consequence. in his philosophic writings, we see him as a
rigid follower of no school of philosophy but rather as an inde-

pendent thinker, a moral philosopher who was interested in, and influenced by, the teachings of the different schools. Philosophic thoughts that suit him Seneca willingly takes from any source— from the Peripatetics and the Epicureans as readily as from the Stoics. He often refers to Aristotle, Chrysippus, Democritus, Epicurus, Plato, Quintus Sextius, Thales, Theophrastus, and Zeno.

But his eclecticism is still more wide-ranging. Although he appears, in *Epistle* 88, to reject almost all of the "liberal studies" (astronomy, grammar, history, mathematics, music, poetry) as not contributing directly to philosophy and virtue, yet Seneca, like Plato before him, does *not* avoid major literary figures in his writings. He refers to or quotes Vergil 119 times, Cicero 30 times, Ovid 28, Homer 23; and he is widely read in historians, citing a number of times Callisthenes, Livy, Asinius Pollio, Sallust, and Timagenes. It should hardly be necessary to add that his imitations in the tragedies reveal his considerable familiarity with the great Greek playwrights, Aeschylus, Sophocles, and Euripides.

Most of all, it is in his writings themselves, their content, their texture, and their traditions, that Seneca most fully demonstrates he broad expansiveness of his quest for knowledge and understanding. As we noted before, he wishes to avoid enslavement to narrow doctrines and commandments: "I have surrendered myself to no one, I am branded with no one's name. I trust the judgment of great men, but I also claim something for my own. For these men have bequeathed to us not unalterable inventions, but rather problems to be investigated (*quaerenda*) . . ." (*Ep.* 45.4). Perhaps the most significant word here is *quaerenda;* Seneca is genuinely and humanely concerned with broad "problems" and *quaestiones* of the creation itself. Since God reveals himself as a spirit in the universe, upon the planet, within Nature and within Man, Seneca's studies range in every one of these places. He had, of course, pursued at the outset of his career a legal practice (*Ep.* 49.2), had reputedly traveled to Egypt, had taken an interest in farming and vine-growing (*Ep.* 104.6; 112.1–2; *N.Q.* 3.7.1), and had risen to great stature in the political world of Rome. Critics frequently discover this broad range of his interests in the very texture of his writings. Thus, one may recognize the influence of rhetoric and declamation in his prose,[69] discern the influence of Greek ideas upon his thought,[70] detect the contemplative strain in him that is concerned with psychology and one's "intériorité,"[71] or assess his long-continued interest in astronomy.[72] Several critics have discussed in his writings what emerges as a deep interest in nature and an acute sensitivity for the beauties of the natural world.[73]

VI   *Range of Interests*

Such a broad range of interests and "problems" for investigation is most clearly revealed in the content of his individual works. Thus, his writings include the literary tragedies, the conversational epistles to Lucilius, a number of epigrams, and the witty and satirical Menippean satire, the *Apocolocyntosis*. His *Natural Questions* displays him surveying the phenomena of nature, the tides of the Nile, the nature of lightning and of earthquakes. His sense of courtliness and of honor lead him to write a book of "duties" and obligations, concerned with the receiving and bestowing of Benefits. His interest in politics induces him to advise the monarch on the uses of Clemency, and his concern for human suffering motivates him to devise for the aggrieved a number of *consolationes*. In ethics, certainly, he is much attracted to a variety of problems: how to accept and utilize the shortness of life, how to endeavor, in an era of unrest, to acquire tranquillity of mind— not to mention separate investigation of the nature of Providence, Leisure, the Happy Life.

His productivity and compass are still more impressive if we remember the host of other subjects Seneca undertook to study and to write about in works that are no longer extant: his poetry, studies of India and of religious cults in Egypt, his orations and exhortations, his studies of matrimony and of friendship, and his scientific studies of minerals and stones and fish.

For the great and repeated lesson of Senecan study was that "it was natural of one to extend his mind outward to the vast universe":

The human soul is great and noble; it tolerates no restrictions save those shared with God. First of all, it does not accept a lowly home, an Ephesus or an Alexandria, or even a city more densely populated or more handsomely contrived; the soul's dwelling encompasses the whole circle of the universe, this entire vault which encloses land and sea and air. . . . Moreover, the soul does not allow itself to be confined to a particular time. "All the years," it says, "are mine; no age is closed to great minds; no era is inaccessible to thought." (*Ep.* 102.21–22)

Seneca's was one such mind that sought to reach out—to all knowledge, to all seasons, to every age. As such, he was one of the few intellects in the increasingly grim period of empire that was not intimidated into narrow confines, to silence, or dullness. Seneca, at one point in his epistles, seeking to assuage Lucilius' fear of death, compares man's life to that of the lamp: "All humans are lighted and extinguished; we suffer somewhat while aglow, but at either end there is deep tranquillity" (*Ep.* 54.5). But even more important is the light of the lamp when it is burning; for Seneca everywhere encourages the laying on of more fuel, the increasing illumination and enlightenment that one's life can bring. With such an attitude, it is no wonder that Seneca lent a torch, all the brighter for his having lived, to the optimistic Renaissance in Europe fourteen hundred years after his own blazing lamp had gone out.

CHAPTER 4

Tragedies of Blood

NOWHERE is Seneca's influential light more clearly ablaze than among the playwrights of the Renaissance and the Elizabethan age. The outstanding position that he held in Europe's revival of learning and, consequently, his inordinate influence upon modern drama has long been a commonplace and is well explored in a number of studies on Seneca and Elizabethan tragedy.[1]

Yet in spite of the high esteem which Seneca's tragedies enjoyed in the fifteenth, sixteenth, and seventeenth centuries, a number of recent critics, failing to analyze Seneca's artistry and originality, but rather constantly, wearisomely comparing his dramas with Greek originals, have left us a considerable body of hostile criticism.[2] They have condemned his excessive use of rhetoric, mythology, epigram, his employment of the bloody and the horrible upon the stage, his penchant for the sensational, his lack of genuine dramatic force. These critics have failed to observe, with T. S. Eliot, that "the proper approach to [an] appreciation and enjoyment [of Seneca] is not by comparison and contrast—to which, in his case, criticism is violently tempted—but by isolation. . . . Such comparisons . . . magnify the defects and obscure the merits of the Senecan tragedy. . . . Seneca is wholly himself; what he attempted he executed, he created his own genre."[3] In order to illustrate this newly developed genre, to reveal Seneca's originality and art, this chapter will analyze two of his most popular plays: the *Medea* and the *Phaedra*.

I *The* Medea

We must begin by observing, first, precisely in what ways Senecan tragedy is unique, different from the Greek tradition. A reading of the *Medea*, for instance, should make these differences apparent.

82

Where Greek tragedy had become fulsome, Seneca's is spare. Where it had been full of action, here there is declamation. Dialogue is replaced by monologue (often suggestive of the Elizabethan "soliloquy"). And scenes are trimmed mercilessly.

We notice as well that time in Senecan drama virtually stands still. Characters never develop; they remain ever the same. Thus the Nurse in the *Medea* solemnly recommends patience and flight throughout; that's all she has to say. The chorus responds most typically—happy at the prospect of a wedding, fearful of Medea. There is no tricky rhetorical Jason here as there was in Euripides, with cunning pseudo-arguments and insinuating roundabout explanations. He claims fear of Creon, but he proceeds mechanically to the wedding, almost as if he enjoyed it. He claims to love his sons. but even here we are not certain, since at the close he recommends that Corinthians set fire to his house, and would destroy everyone within in order to destroy Medea. Medea herself is virtually a constant in the play: in the Prologue, she appears in a towering rage, and she continues haltingly, frantically, in precisely that selfsame emotional state throughout.

We likewise observe that the Euripidean messenger describes the cruel deaths of Creusa and Creon in detail; Seneca condenses them to a mere few lines on the general fire at the palace. Where Euripides could employ subtle satiric tactics, so that the Chorus of Corinthians even come to sympathize with Medea (most unnatural and unpatriotic), here the Chorus is aloof, Medea left isolated and alone. Where Euripides added notes about the Athenian king taking Medea as an exile (thereby making Athenians feel a bit uneasy), Seneca eliminates such scenes. For Seneca is concerned neither with motives to action nor with action itself— but with that garish in-between state, the emotions themselves.

Such raw emotions are few and paramount. Jason dramatizes a "dishonorable" fear (*timor:* lines 433–38, 493–94, 516–19, 529). Most of all, Medea, who looms monomaniacally and singularly upon the scene, dramatizes wrath—an ire that is almost sublime in its frenzy—a frenzy often in the play meant to indicate pure madness. Her hesitations about slaughtering her sons are perfunctory. Moreover, the process of butchery is extended, since she murders one within, only to carry the other upon the roof before his demise. She is arch-attestor to vehemence, to barbarian witchcraft, venom, and furor.

It is precisely such singularity of raw, poisonous emotion that
has earned Senecan tragedy its reputation as the "Tragedy of
Blood."⁴ Characters like Medea are uniformly—almost incessantly
—intent upon murder and mayhem, and Seneca is particularly
attracted to such myths of violence, as his use of the bloody stories
of *Thyestes, Oedipus,* and *Hercules Furens* will attest. Such plays
typically conclude, at the catastrophe, with virtually a savage
bloodbath of revenge, assassination, and destruction.⁵ Moreover,
Seneca's trim and terse dramatic structuring of his plays merely
enhances our sense of this savage state. He is particularly known,
in his plays, for concise, laconic choruses, for stichomythic (tart,
epigrammatic) contentions among pairs of characters, and for a
garish cluster of mood-creating conventions—rash invocations of
deities, sudden and splenetic curses, vast rhetorical hyperboles,
intensely reflective soliloquies or "asides." His characters' speeches
(and Medea is noteworthy here) are taut but extensive, nervously
cumulative outbursts of highly declamatory and figurative assev-
erations. For Senecan situations almost instinctively climb to a
high and horrible rhetorical pitch, and his stage is ever replete
with the threat or the actuality of ghosts, apparitions, monsters,
dragons, curses, black magic, and madness itself.

For such reasons, and for their repeated representation of
unique and vicious emotions at fever pitch, Seneca's dramas cannot be read, quite (at least in the Greek sense), as plays. There is
no interlocking "chain" of events and inevitable unfolding of action which Aristotle speaks about with reference, particularly, to
Sophocles. Instead, his piece is a steel glass, portraying pictures in
clipped segments—each picture being but a graphic portrayal in
little of a single phase of Medean madness. His plays must be
witnessed, then, as an intense perusal of the same thing: a tone
poem intricately relaying, again and again, a predominant theme.
For this reason, his so-called dramas are closer to Pindaric odes,
to declamations, to elegiac laments. For all of them develop and
explore the thread of a single mood.

This does not mean, of course, that Seneca's plays are "inferior"
to the Greeks'; they are inferior, one supposes, if judged by Greek
standards.⁶ Yet, as I have sought to show, Seneca's drama is
hardly dramatic, but something distinctly other than tragic theater
in the accepted Hellenic sense. Therefore, it cannot be said that
his plays suffer or are weak; they are intense representations of

violent emotional moods, caught and displayed like still lifes of a cataclysm. The single-mindedness of such presentations is, admittedly, a vigorous, a rich, perhaps even a stifling dish. His is not a dessert that will be to most men's taste.

But his decoction certainly reveals a unique taste. Nor can he be faulted for lack of artistic coherence.[7] For, within his pictorial genre, there is unifying artistry enough. For one thing, Seneca in such a pictorial art is fond of terse, disparate juxtapositioning. Thus, Medea's opening speech is a soliloquy of violence—she appeals to the gods for aid in obtaining vengeance and calls upon Lucina, Minerva, and the sun-god, speaking of torches and fire. Immediately afterward, the unwitting happy Chorus enters and delivers a speech of almost precisely the same length! Yet its content is emotionally the oppostite from Medea's harangue—though, notwithstanding, the topics are, ironically, the same! Thus, they wish to celebrate the good cheer of Jason's marriage to Creusa, and appeal, as Medea had done, to Lucina, to Minerva, and to the sun-god, mentioning the fires of heaven and the wedding torches.

This kind of almost wickedly contrived contrast is a strong feature in Senecan composition. And similar to it is the continuance of such imagery throughout the play. Thus, Medea repeatedly appeals to underworld deities, to torches and to fires.

Moreover, Seneca, because of his method of brusquely sculpting each scene, is able to stand far aloof from the drama. And he imposes upon the play a unifying theme of balance and significant circularity. Thus, it is urged repeatedly that Medea, as the slayer of her own brother and of King Pelias, is certainly expected to be criminal. At the last, when she slaughters her own two sons, the imagery makes it clear that she has come full-circle, that these two deaths "atone" for—and evenly "match"—the earlier two. Even Medea recognizes, to some extent, the fulfillment of a "pattern": "Now, now I have recovered my sceptre, my brother, my father; and the Colchians hold again the spoil of the golden fleece; my kingdom is returned, my ravished virginity restored" (*Medea* 982–84).

Seneca establishes thereby the fullness and completeness of Medea's journey. Yet the last irony is surely not Medea's, but our own. Poor Medea has raged and insisted upon "revenge" throughout the play, and certainly believes, toward the close, that she has accomplished that revenge: as she has said—this is "my day" (meaning the one "day" Creon has granted her prior to her being exiled, but also indicating her clear sense of the fulfillment and "satisfaction" of her retaliation).[8] Yet the last irony makes it clear that the revenge has been taken upon herself: the spirit of her murdered brother, the fiery serpents and shades set loose by her magic run away with her, escape her control, and ultimately control her. Thus, the dead brother and the Hecatean spirits ("furies" they are at times appropriately termed; cf. *Erinyes*), in forcing Medea to murder her sons, are taking vengeance upon her! In a bitterly ironic sense that she does not fully perceive, she has come full circle: for Medea's latest murders balance and avenge the earlier ones, and, in a terribly barren sense, she returns to the state she had been in at Colchis, prior to her flight with the Argonauts. Murders with murders are near allied; yet such slaughter of kin, of extensions of one's self, are Pyrrhic victories, pathetic riots beyond even her control. So, the last grim leer and laugh are upon Medea. And the audience is made to sense very sharply that the amassing of violent emotions, the utilization of evil spirits, or the vicious murdering of human victims can become habitual: Medea bereft is Medea still. And further vengeance and savagery and atonement will ever attend her.[9]

II   *The* Phaedra

Much of the shift in emphasis in Seneca's tragedy, placing new weight upon human villainy, can be most readily detected by comparison of Euripides' *Hippolytus* with Seneca's *Phaedra*. In Euripides, the entire framing device had placed the blame upon the gods; Venus, jealous of Hippolytus' single-minded devotion to Diana the Huntress, contrives Phaedra's fatal passion for her stepson—all to bring him into ill repute. In Seneca's version, on the contrary, there are no such machinations of the gods; Phaedra herself, like Medea, generated her own passion and villainy. Her love for Hippolytus is exemplary of irrational lust and passion—elevated, as is so common with Seneca, to madness and frenzy. Theseus, too, is more signally implicated than in Euripides; for here Theseus has been away from his wife for four years—off in the underworld seeking a brazen adultery with Persephone, the Queen of Hades, whereas in the Greek play Theseus is away on a mere business trip. Both Phaedra and Hippolytus in the Senecan version are hard and determined, bent upon self-willed and "unnatural" excess. The Nurse, too, remains but one more character "dishonored" by her fond devotion to Phaedra's every wish. Even Hippolytus is not merely a high-minded "victim" of the triangle, but a man given over to extravagant imbalance and hatred of the entirety of womankind.

Nor is such intemperance excused on the ground of Hippolytus' illegitimate birth as it is in the Euripidean version; for here Seneca clearly implies a normative marriage between Theseus and Antiope. Thus, Hippolytus is "naturally" accountable for his immoderation. He is excessively—even fatally—violent concerning his chastity. "I hate them all, I fear, flee, curse them all. Be it reason, be it natural disposition, be it dire rage, to hate them is my pleasure" (*Phaedra* 566–68). His response to Phaedra's offer of love is one of thundering outrage; he calls upon the gods to witness *the worst of women*, and threatens to cut her down upon the spot. The point is, certainly, that Senecan characters are excessive in the extreme. They almost range in some precise "order" of evil. Phaedra is worst, but just beneath her stand Theseus and the Nurse, and at some little distance beyond, Hippolytus himself. Phaedra, openly maligning Hippolytus as a ravisher when Theseus returns, is most the conniver and base deceiver. She offers a final confession, before killing herself, but it is not a speech containing the slightest sense of remorse: she assaults Theseus himself as a bringer of death and ill fortune and merely cannot continue living in her distraught state of love for Hippolytus. Passionately she lived in this play; passionately she dies.

The Chorus, as in the *Medea,* plays its usual aloof but informed role. It is true that in the *Phaedra* the Chorus is more dramatic than in the *Medea;* it speaks upon occasion with the other characters—but has little character of its own. It remains detached, its membership unknown. Its members speak directly of love and of the "stepmother"; they musically, as it were, enhance the play's themes, but are hardly part of the action. They do know of the lies and plots with which the palace abounds (as they did not in Euripides' play) and they are all the more shocking for refraining from utilizing this knowledge—especially when Theseus returns and is beguiled to slaughter his son as a result of Phaedra's guile. Instead, like many of Aeschylus' Choruses, this one offers sad, lyrical, and almost inept songs of frustration: Hippolytus is beauty itself, excelling even that of the gods (!), but such beauty cannot last—and is its own ill reward. "Cast a glance over the ages: Few men have possessed beauty without suffering for it" (*Phaedra* 820–21). Or again, a choral song echoing the lament of Job observes that mighty nature appears so full of order in the universe, and yet goes haywire in the affairs of men; for evil prospers and the good expire: "Fortune in disarray governs human affairs and blindly scatters her gifts, favoring the foul; dreadful lust conquers blameless men, fraud in the lofty palace prevails" (*Phaedra* 978–82). The Chorus, as an aloof and perplexed and pained spectator, views the carnage and carnival of passions played out upon the stage, attempting to register some feeble protest and yearning to hammer some form of meaningfulness from the anvil of dreadful events. They hardly succeed and certainly do not act; yet they render a musical continuity to the dire drama portraying vicious events.

But the last melodic meditation, just referred to above, concerning nature's apparent inversion, is the significant motif in this play: "Gloomy virtue heaps perverse rewards upon rectitude; hateful poverty pursues the chaste, and the adulterer, vicious, potent, predominates" (*Phaedra* 985–88). This vision of virtue heaping perversity (*virtus perversa tulit*) is a recurring melodic line in the play. It constitutes the *topos* that E. R. Curtius designates "the world upside down"[10] and is pre-eminent in the *Phaedra*. Indeed, such a pervasive sense of nature overturned is the dominant artistic motif shaping the drama's form and course.

From the very outset, this theme is emphasized in the roles of the central characters. Hippolytus is the adherent of but a single goddess, Diana. His excessive devotion to a single deity is understood as a monomaniacal perverseness, exemplified in Hippolytus' extreme position in hating women, glorifying his own chastity, and shunning city and civilized society. Theseus, too, is conceived of in Seneca's play as the embodiment of another roadway to the perverse. He has, together with Pirithous, dared four years before to venture into the underworld, an act unnatural enough; but to that he adds his intention of an adulterous amour with Hades' queen. And Phaedra, of course, is overcome by an incestuous passion for her stepson.

Moreover, the play is filled with allusions to the *past* of Theseus' and Phaedra's families; it is made abundantly evident that these unnatural vices are "family" diseases: "offspring returns to its source and degenerate blood recreates its primal stock" (*Phaedra* 907–8). Hippolytus' mother Antiope had been a famed Amazon— a race of women celebrated for their "unbalanced" topsy-turviness, as the meaning of the Greek word Amazon (without breast) implies. A fierce tribe of warlike women in Scythia, they exiled males or put young boys to death. It is no wonder that the son of such a mother savagely rejects the opposite sex and pursues a career of warlike hunting in the forests. Similarly, Theseus' backgrounds are significant. He had cruelly abandoned Phaedra's sister, Ariadne, at Naxos, despite the fact of her love and devotion, which had virtually saved his life in his adventures in Minos' court. In addition, he had put to death his own Amazonian wife, Antiope, and his carelessness in announcing his successful return to Athens had caused his own father, Aegeus, to take his life. Nor does the play fail to mention a number of times that Aegeus had taken the barbarian Medea to wife. Of a like strain is Phaedra's kin. Her mother, Pasiphae, was renowned for her unnatural intercourse with Poseidon's bull, resulting in the birth of the monstrous Minotaur, which Theseus later had slain.

Such backgrounds are, of course, common knowledge as the stuff of mythology; but Seneca makes certain that these tangled unnatural skeins are repeatedly alluded to and exaggerated in his dramatic poem. They are made to take their place beside other strains of this dominant motif that courses throughout the play. Thus, in an initial choral ode of considerable importance, the almost insane predominance of Venus and Love is forcefully related: Zeus, for love of Leda, turned himself into the swan; for love of Europa, he assumed the shape of the bull. Selene, the moon-goddess, similarly abandoned her accustomed role in the heavens to pursue the handsome shepherd Endymion. And, most unnatural of all, the great Hercules, out of love for Omphale, allows himself to put aside his lion skin and famous club and to be bedecked in woman's garb and occupied at the spindle (*Phaedra* 317–24).

Ironically, in the heat of his hatred for women, Hippolytus later treats the love of man for woman as something similarly unnatural: "You will mix fire with water and the turbulent Syrtes will promise calm waters to ships, Tethys from the shore of Hesperia in the farthest west will bring the dawn, and wolves gaze fondly among the deer before I shall be overcome and mildly tolerate a woman" (*Phaedra* 568–73). And when Phaedra finally reveals her love to him, Hippolytus again is overwhelmed with a righteous sense of unnatural vice and cries out for the world to turn backward in its course: "Let the sky be shaken and dashed to ruin and shroud the day in black clouds, and let the stars, turned backwards and contorted, move obliquely. And, chiefest star, radiant Sun, do you behold mankind's wickedness? Turn off your light and flee to darkness" (*Phaedra* 674–79).

And when Theseus learns of Hippolytus' so-called ravishment of his wife, he is overwhelmed by a sense of his son's perverse Amazonian inheritance. "O hideous race unsubdued by laws of a better country! Even the wild beasts themselves avoid incestuous love, and an intuitive sense of shame regulates every species" (*Phaedra* 911–14). And shortly afterward, when he has utilized his last of three "wishes" to instruct Neptune to destroy his son, Theseus is fully aware that his curse is hideously unnatural; he commands it, though he expects the world to overturn as a result. "Now keep your word. Father, do you delay? Why are the waters still silent? Now obscure the night, while winds drive black clouds everywhere, snatch away the stars and the heavens, pour out the sea, arouse the massy sea, and summon the swollen waves from Ocean itself" (*Phaedra* 953–58). And, of course, the apex of this unnatural strain, so heavily emphasized in this play, occurs when Neptune's monstrous sea-bull emerges from the depths of the sea and precipitates Hippolytus' destruction.

In this unnatural climate, it is ironically appropriate that a "bull" should destroy the offspring of Theseus—for who was it but Theseus who had slain the Minoan bull and facilitated the capture of the Marathonian Bull? Moreover, the imagery of Cretan perversions is united with Hippolytus' enjoyment of the ox hunt. And above all, ironically, in the final scene of Hippolytus' life, the bull is unnaturally a denizen of the sea, and the hunter is made captive by the hunted.

Indeed, Seneca has carefully plotted his drama to underscore and to enhance this web of inversion and inhumanity. The opening speech by Hippolytus, praising the pleasures of the hunt at great length (lines 1–84), has often been considered by critics to be unnecessarily extended and digressive. But it is important that Hippolytus be "placed" as the perfervid "hunter" in this play. To be sure, the speech emphasizes his almost unearthly *idée fixe,* but it also becomes all the more significant, in terms of reversal and perversion, when, at the close, as we have observed, the hunter is hunted down. Furthermore, the hunting imagery is never laid aside during the play. Phaedra herself, in an ironic reversal, threatens to hunt the hunter: "If he flees, I'll follow him across the very sea" (*Phaedra* 241). "Though he cling to the tops of the snow-covered hill, though he trample the jagged rocks with agile foot, still I am determined to follow him over mountains and through deep woods" (*Phaedra* 233–35). Even when Hippolytus has learned of her incestuous love and has violently denounced her, she still persists in the chase. "I shall follow you even through fire, through the raging sea, over rocks and streams which the torrential waters sweep along; wherever you go, there shall I in my madness pursue (*Phaedra* 700–702). And this maddening hunt reaches its apex in Phaedra's final speech when she intends to take her own life and still pursue the shade of the departed Hippolytus. Distractedly she addresses him: "With this hand will I pay the penalty to you and thrust the sword into my wicked breast, releasing Phaedra both from crime and from life, and in my madness I shall pursue you across waters, across the lakes of Tartarus, over the Styx, over rivers of fire" (*Phaedra* 1176–80). To the last, undismayed, undiminished, Phaedra's paradoxical and distorted passion haunts herself and hunts another.

The final instance of Seneca's artful imagery portraying this unnatural world is provided by Theseus. Thunderstruck at Phaedra's last confession and overwhelmed by a sense of his own guilt in his son's demise, he calls out hoarsely for the underworld spirits and monsters of the deep to close this unnatural drama by seizing the unnatural filicide (lines 1201–6). And in these last, troubling moments of the play, Theseus finally perceives the grotesque irony of his case: "Is it to this I have returned? Was a path from Hades to the upper world granted me only that I might witness two murders and two funerals, that I, bereft of wife and son, might ignite the funeral pyres of both with a single torch?" (*Phaedra* 1213–16). It is the climax of this miserable portrayal of inversion and debasement. Hippolytus the hunter has been hunted down. The supposedly ravished Phaedra is the ravisher. And now, Theseus has returned from the land of the dead—only to pervert the land of the living with death. His new life bears witness only to funereal bereavement. Hercules had rescued Theseus, he now perceives, and brought him back to a light that is but darkness (line 1217). On this grotesque note of expiration, revolution, and ironic inversion, Seneca's apt picture of an unnatural world in his drama draws to a close.

III Seneca's "Fearful" Drama and Its Influence

It is precisely this sounding-of-the-depths of incessant misery that signally rendered Seneca's tragedies influential in the Renaissance. For his conception of tragedy differs considerably from the Greek norm. The role of "fate" is by far more significant among the Greeks. Thus, as one observer has noted, Greek tragedy and Nordic sagas all too often represent heroic man caught in a hopeless situation, caught, as it were, between two conflicting duties, between two discordant choices—and either choice is wrong.[11] This is, for instance, the position in which an Oedipus or an Antigone is likely to find himself or herself. And traditional criticism of Greek tragedy has, rightly, perceived this dilemma. Thus, Aristotle, in the *Poetics*, appears to picture the audience as captivated by two opposing responses, *pity* and *fear*.[12] One feels a sympathetic attraction to the tragic hero, as well as a fearful repulsion away from him. This kind of "balance" of contending emotions is most typically achieved in Sophoclean drama.[13]

It is, however, perfectly reasonable to consider dramas that "break" this harmonious contention. A tragedy, for instance, that emphasizes "pity" would eventually, like English Restoration "heroic" drama, move toward a tender romantic empathy and a high-sounding melodrama. On the other hand, Senecan drama emphasized "fear"—the emotion of shock and revulsion, withdrawal and dismay. Characters simply do not present themselves as equally admirable and reprehensible. Instead, they foster in us a sense of unpleasantness and disapprobation. It was such "fearful" drama that influenced much of Elizabethan and Jacobean performance. Thomas Kyd's *Spanish Tragedy*, Marlowe's *Jew of Malta*, John Marston's *Malcontent*, Shakespeare's *Troilus and Cressida* and *Coriolanus*, and particularly John Webster's *Duchess of Malfi* and *White Devil* dramatize a savagery and carnage that is "fearful" in the extreme.

Moreover, Seneca is "modern" precisely insofar as he would challenge the "heroism" of someone like Theseus. He would,

doubtless, agree with the modern novelist Michael Ayrton, who views Theseus as renowned merely for cruelty, impetuosity, and riot. Ayrton's Daedalus speaks of Theseus as criminal:

. . . a relative of mine. He has become very celebrated and is much admired for his treachery to Ariadne, . . . for slaying the Minotaur, with her help, . . . [and] for his accidental—if it was accidental—destruction of his own father by negligence in the matter of the color of the sail, and other heroic acts. Perhaps the most famous of all his exploits is the victory he achieved over a group of women, a large number of whom were killed in battle with him. Altogether, my kinsman Theseus . . . was a murderous hero, which is the common kind. . . . This must be accepted, for killing, like so many destructive activities, is unavoidable to the uncreative. It is their principal demonstration of power.[14]

And Seneca, for all of his language of "insanity" or "madness," does not portray his characters as being exonerated by fatality; they are not murderous and depraved by *fiat* and destiny. It would be a mistaken determination to consider Senecan characters hostages of fortune, victims of *moira* and circumstance. Rather, his dramas insist upon viewing human beings, not as victimized predators of a perjured, manifest destiny, but as ultimately responsible for their own actions.[15]

No one will claim, it should seem clear, that Hippolytus is coerced to lead his life as sportsman in the chase. Nor would we insist that Theseus sought out Hades by another's will. But Phaedra is the signal case. The Chorus claims that all are determined victims of Love: "The monster of the mad sea loves and so do Lucanian bulls; Love claims all nature for itself; nothing is immune, and hatred perishes at Love's command" (*Phaedra* 351–54). And Phaedra urges just this point, that she is victimized by the inevitable magnetism of love: "No daughter of Minos experienced a love that was mild; wickedness ever attends it" (*Phaedra* 127–28). But the Nurse insists to her that one "elects" one's crimes: "wickedness is greater than a monstrosity; for you impute monstrosities to fate, wickedness to character" (*Phaedra* 143–44). And Phaedra concurs (lines 177–78). Phaedra's passion is one that she must displace or curb, and she is unwilling to have it so. Significantly, these characters are not merely, as in ancient myth, "fated" and "cursed" to lead wretched, predetermined lives, the victims of external and divine mandate. They are presented as people capable of will and self-control, but who have given themselves over to indulgence and an almost insane cultivation of pleasures and passions. They are capable of being better persons, but will not be so. Parts are being distributed in life, and they have selected the worst roles.

Consequently, Senecan tragedy consists of the fearful presentation of self-willed vice. But it would be incorrect, I think, for us to conclude that Seneca the philosopher's plays are for this reason rhetorical "messages"—thinly veiled discursive and doctrinal lessons in "proper conduct." On the contrary, like most great art, the dramas are fictive and poetic, not editorial; they present and convey meaning by actions and patterns of action; they do not deliver meaning by proclamation, assertion, or debate. The actions and the patterns of action *are* the plays' meanings, as I hope we have seen from examining the *Medea* and the *Phaedra;* and Seneca is far from being the mere orator or message-monger; his concern, as it is for every significant artist, is with the fullness and richness of his artful work. Seneca, like Demodocus, would cherish his art as inspiring song. History and personal life might tremble and pass, but art and creation are prolonged. *Ars longa, vita brevis.*

Tell me why you weep in your heart and lament when you hear about the adversities of the Argives and the Greeks. The gods so arranged it, spinning the destruction of men, so that for posterity a Song shall remain.[16]

CHAPTER 5

Irony and Wit

SENECA the philosopher is best known to us for his ethical precepts, his influential tragedies, his role as courtier in the Claudian and Neronian Age. But above all, we regard him as Stoic moralist and most frequently associate him with a level-headed, determined, even grim moral earnestness. We think of this Seneca as one who extolled humanitarianism in an era of slavery, stoutly championed clemency in a period of stark brutality, urged Stoical self-restraint in a society of effete lasciviousness, and potent frankness in a world of adulation and obsequiousness. In the world of Rome that was crumbling and burning, he appears to be a staunch pillar of the Stoic Porch.

But there is another side to the philosopher, a playful open-mindedness reminiscent of the Cynic orators and Horace: "And should you ask what leader, what philosophic school I obey: Having sworn allegiance to the words of no master, I am carried, like a guest, wherever the winds drive me. At one moment I become active and plunge into the tides of public affairs, a guardian and strict attendant of true virtue; at another, I stealthily relapse into the precepts of Aristippus and try to adapt circumstances to myself, not myself to circumstances,"[1] Horace could boast. Likewise, Seneca in philosophy calls for a free wafting of the intellectual spirit: "Shall I not tread in the footsteps of my predecessors? I shall, indeed, use the old road, but if I come upon one that is shorter and easier, I shall pursue it" (*Ep.* 33.11).[2] In practice, he jocularly wields this principle of open-mindedness, and in so doing at times shocks his auditors, as, for example, when he draws a picture of the strict Stoic embracing the maxims of—Epicurus.[3]

I   *Senecan Dualism and the Modern Dilemma*

No one can be more ethically in earnest when Seneca argues, as in the *De Ira,* in favor of the disciplined life and control of the

95

passions. And yet, no one is more readily aware that playfulness, a certain relaxation, the applauding of "holiday," is essential to the intellectual life.

The mind must not be kept taut, at the same tension, but must be un-wound by diversions. Socrates did not blush to play with little children and Cato, when weary of public affairs, relaxed his mind with wine, and Scipio swayed his victorious, military body to the sound of music. . . . (*De Tranq. An.* 17.4)

The mind must be indulged and from time to time must be given relax-ation which provides it with food and power. (*De Tranq. An.* 17.8)

Games also will be helpful; for moderate pleasure relaxes and tempers the mind. (*De Ira* 2.20.3)

Sometimes we should even go so far as to become intoxicated, allowing drink, not to take complete control, but to have some effect on us. (*De Tranq. An.* 17.8)

Moreover, conflicting responses to Seneca dramatize his hetero-geneous personality. A Montaigne can overstress Seneca's virtue and wisdom—viewing the man wholly as *philosopher;*[4] whereas a Shaftesbury can regard Seneca's philosophical role as alien, and adjudge him a *born courtier.*[5]

Whence this contradiction, this conflict of opinion? The dispute is capable of mediation, and we might proffer a solution: the Stoics had ever pronounced their goal to be, like Robert Frost's union of his vocation with his avocation,[6] the realization of the Platonic ideal of uniting *vita activa* and *vita contemplativa.*[7] Cyn-ics also proclaimed such a unified ideal, but Diogenes and Bion too often appear a bit more like radicals and rebels than like ra-tional activists. Among the Stoics, however, the name of Seneca exemplifies most clearly the success of such a union; Seneca him-self asserts: "Virtue is divided into two parts, into contemplation of truth and into action" (*Ep.* 94.45). And again: "Who will deny that virtue should test her progress by deeds, and should not only consider what ought to be done but also apply herself to doing it" (*De Otio* 6.3). If Seneca values the private virtues of leisure and tranquillity of mind, he likewise studied the public virtues of mercy and the courtly conferring and accepting of benefactions.

He advises retirement frequently in the *Epistulae Morales* to Lucilius,[8] yet he also warns of the dangers of contemplative philosophy.[9] Seneca endorses both lives; he prefers richness, variety, fullness.

In fact, it is just such a variety of traits to which Tacitus refers. Seneca represents for the historian the *bonae artes*[10] and a distinctive *ingenium*.[11] But Seneca also signifies to him courtly eloquence and *comitas honesta*.[12] Even at the moment of his death, the philosopher is depicted in the *Annals* as combining these several qualities in his last discussion with friends: chatting with them "now conversationally, now intensely and urgently."[13]

As a matter of fact, in his writings Seneca constantly revives the debate between *vita activa* and *vita contemplativa;* the dichotomy is never resolved. For Seneca never makes an overt choice; now he advocates one path, now the other. He is well aware of the paradox that pristine Stoics (Zeno, Cleanthes, Chrysippus) recommended the public life without having lived it themselves (*De Tranq. An.* 1.10). In the last analysis, Seneca urges the Aristotelian "mean" between the two ways of life. Nor is such mediation a mere platitude or verbal sleight; Seneca very distinctly acclaims action *and* thought; he deftly plants one foot in each world.[14]

Actually, such dualism—between the cavalier and the philosopher, between public action and private reflection, between serious discourse and *spoudaiogeloion* (earnest jesting)—typifies the man, adding a complex dimension to his character and his thought. And in reality, such dichotomies mirror many a dilemma of modern man. Senecan divisions and revisions are of a kind that, empathetically, we can understand. For the modern, the twentieth-century impetus also has been directed toward man's striving to attain simultaneously a complex number of points of view, a quest for what might be called the life of irony. One thinks of John Keats's artistic endeavor to transcend the self: his very conception of "negative capability" is the artist's ideal of escaping from the self, of discovering the ability to project oneself outward into a number of varied, and even contradictory, fictional characters and states of mind. When such an ironic state is achieved, the poet's character literally "has no self—it is everything and nothing—It has no character—it enjoys light and shade; it lives in gusto, be it foul or fair, high or low, rich or poor, mean or elevated—It has as much delight in conceiving an Iago as an Imogen.

What shocks the virtuous philosopher, delights the camelion Poet."[15] Keats is in fact describing that classical artistic practice known as *decorum personae*.[16] And it is precisely such classical decorum that innumerable moderns feel they lack. Such moderns strive mightily to escape from a romantic imprisonment within the self, to regain the lost art of irony.

William Butler Yeats may serve as a prime instance of this struggle in our century. Throughout his career, Yeats sought more and more to lift himself out of himself, to transcend the Romantic fuzziness and sentimentality of his early poetry. As a result, he came to create in his later poetry "dialogues," in which a fictional Robartes debates with a fictional Aherne, a Crazy Jane debates with her bishop, and Yeats himself manages in his finest poetry the *agon* between his self and soul.[17]

Jung has postulated that without "tensions" and conflict within the self there would be no progress of individual or society to "wider and higher consciousness."[18] And increasingly moderns have sought to confront their conflicts, seeking greater and ever greater awareness of themselves and the world. Such internal conflict is clearly evident in the writings of Seneca himself, as we have seen, linking him firmly with much that colors the modern mood. It is significant, for instance, that Seneca gives an extended and painful account of that modern malady, "ennui" (*taedium*) (*De Tranq. An.* 2.10 ff.).[19] And, like present-day Existentialists, Seneca argued for a recognition of the inherent virtue found in adversity,[20] and for the necessity of confronting the "absurd" or irrational nature of human society.[21] But most existential of all is Seneca's insistence that a man must come face to face with the possibilities of suicide, that man must seriously consider such a last stroke of rebellion from life, such a rejection of life itself.[22] Like the Existentialist, he encourages this frank confrontation with death, a virtual, fearful and trembling "dark night of the soul," so that one may *return* from such meditation of suicide with a new existential sense of humanitarian commitment to life.[23]

Thus, in one dialogue, Seneca imagines God speaking to mortals, if with a touch of sarcasm, yet also with a substantial portion of truth: "If you do not wish to fight, you can flee. Therefore, of all things that I considered necessary for you, I made nothing easier than death. I placed life on an inclined plane; you think life is too long drawn out?—only pay attention, and you will see how short and easy is the path that leads to liberty" (*De Prov.* 6.7). The scoffing argument has really sought to urge men to live life, and to scorn or even to admire adversity. And the note of a proud (because hard-won) humanism is distinctly rung: "In this you may surpass God; He is immune to the endurance of evil, you have transcended it" (*De Prov.* 6.6). Man becomes ironic virtually by the sheer pressure and force of his suffering and his skepticism; and the Stoic sage, like a Camus or a Nietzsche, transcends himself by submitting to the larger pattern of nature.

II *Urbanity and Irony*

Seneca is further the ironist in exactly the same fashion that Plato had been: both men derived from the well-to-do classes, both had early experienced the defeat of any ideals they might have had for the philosophical education of a monarch. Further, Seneca knew, as Plato had known before him, that the vision he had of a political universal brotherhood and society of men was merely a vision. Can a philosophical enthusiast ever devote himself politically to an actual Athens or a tangible Carthage? Surely not, he tells us. "But if that state which we envision cannot be found, retirement becomes a necessity for all, because the single ideal that would have been preferable to withdrawal nowhere exists" (*De Otio* 8.3).[24] Yet, at the opposite extreme, Seneca knows that the man who withdraws from political service is too fastidious (*De Otio* 8.1); his haughty and punctilious refinement will end in his isolation from life itself. For in Seneca's view, one *must* lead the active life: "But, to be sure, no day is long to the active man. Let us expand our life; the duty and proof of life is action" (*Ep.* 122.3).

It is just these contradictions, these conflicting points of view in his every work that characterize Senecan irony. It has often perplexed critics why the Ambrosian manuscript containing Senecan writings designates the twelve Moral Essays *Dialogi*. It is indeed true that they are not in any strict sense dialogues at all. One would suggest, however, that it is not merely the presence in their pages of a formal *adversarius* like Paulinus or Serenus or Novatus, but rather their content, the internal shiftings of Senecan point of view, the reversals and second thoughts, that ironically insist upon exploring a topic from its every side, that earn these treatises their name. As Seneca has again and again insisted: "Without an adversary, virtue languishes" (*De Prov.* 2.4).

Thus, Seneca's works consistently affirm the stance of irony, a playful metaphysical seriousness notable only in the more mature literary minds: Homer, Plato, Horace, Dante, Shakespeare, Voltaire, Goethe, Faulkner. It is an irony that also appears only in highly civilized nations, during highly cultured periods. Is not such irony in fact nothing other than *urbanitas:* a civilized and cultivated ease in bearing varieties of wisdom? *Urbanitas*, that very style of polished discrimination in speech, a witty control and elegance that Cicero finds not in Gallic but in Roman orators alone?[25]

Seneca enacts such urbane irony innumerable times. In the *De Vita Beata*, after Seneca the moralist has delivered a long passage of typical Stoic doctrine extolling virtue and the virtuous life to Gallio, an *adversarius* (hypothetically) interrupts the moralist with a long catalogue of accusations: "Why, then, Seneca, if all these words about Stoic virtue be true, do you, Seneca, fail to obey them? Why do you so much value money, vast landholdings, elaborate furnishings, costly goods, studied banquets, hoary wines?" Here the *adversarius* initiates a reversal of the Saturnalian kind; and perhaps at this place we are reminded of the insolence of a Davus lecturing Horace.[26] When this accuser ceases, Seneca literally joins him, adding to the heap of incriminating evidence against himself. "Later on," he even promises, "I shall add to your reproaches and upbraid myself more than you can imagine. . . ." And then, after a pause, Seneca answers, simply: "I am not a *sapiens* and, you'll be glad to know, never will be one" (*De Vita Beata* 17.1–3).

This reply is not merely the "loophole" employed by an invidious pseudo-philosopher or archhypocrite; it is the witty acknowledgment of the truth about human kind. For a moment, the high-flying rhetoric of the moralist halts, and the bird of oratory, with folded wings, plunges to the ground. It is a moment of truth, but it is also a moment of wit; one can almost perceive the twinkling gleam in the Senecan eye. For Seneca knows well enough the laws of jests and laughter: "No one is laughable who can laugh at himself" (*De Cons. Sap.* 17.2). Seneca is a moralist and serious man, but one capable at any moment of seizing a laughing pleasure. He is one, he tells Lucilius, "who used to celebrate January 1st by taking a dip in the canal, since his New Year's resolutions included a leap into the aqueduct as well as reading, writing, and declaiming" (*Ep.* 83.5).

It is precisely Seneca's capacity for playfulness as well as for philosophy, for earnest irony, for risible rationality, that deserves to win for him a companionable chair at our modern table. All too often, we have not set for him a place. All's the more pity that we should miss his company, for Seneca is himself something like the poor Epicureans he again and again so "solicitously" defends: the Epicureans are misunderstood, he exclaims; it is only their outside that appears abandoned, evil, effete. Inside, their doctrine contains matter of worth. Here Seneca offers kindly illustration, by analogy: "Such is the case as when a strong man puts on a woman's gown; your chastity remains, your virility is intact, your body is free from prostitution, but in your hand is a tambourine!" (*De Vita Beata* 13.6).[27] This ironic image, with but little adaptation, may be applied as a description of Seneca himself. And does not the figure, so sharply contrasting outside with inside, remind us of that other famous contrast, Alcibiades' depiction of Socrates as the Silenus statue: ugly on the outside, but revealing inside the epiphany of beautiful gods?[28]

The figures describing Seneca and Socrates are very like. And yet, there is an important difference: the Socratic ugliness was proverbial; what needed emphasis was the rich fund of Socratic beauty of mind beneath the surface. With Seneca, however, the case is reversed; everyone knows of Seneca's moral wisdom; what needs emphasis in our time is the wit in which the wisdom lies hidden.

III *Humor and Paradox*

Humorous tactics are ever present in Seneca's prose. He likes to indulge in a jest, a pun, or an unexpected turn in the argument. In his very first Moral Epistle to Lucilius, it is the tongue-in-cheek wealthy Seneca who shocks his *adversarius* by announcing: "I will give you reasons for my poverty" (*Ep.* 1.4). Or he will commence an epistle with a shocking proposition: "O how hostile to us are the wishes of our parents!" (*Ep.* 60.1). Nor does Seneca exempt even himself from comic assault: he at times turns off all his Stoic dignity, until he appears almost the equal of Henry Fielding's comical Parson Adams. Perhaps the most humorous scene in the

Epistulae Morales is the one which portrays a frightened and sea-sickened Seneca, ludicrously comparing himself to Odysseus, plunging overboard from a ship to flee a storm, and dropping into freezing waters! (*Ep.* 53.1–4). It is these elements of wit and play in Seneca that I should like further to explore.[29] And we can find no better place to begin than with Seneca's employment of paradox.

The pages of Seneca's philosophical prose are invested with numerous traditional Stoic paradoxes.[30] Nonetheless, Seneca is apt frequently to produce what is, even for a Stoic, the distinctive, the unexpected paradox: uncommon opinions unlooked and uncalled for, more jolting to our anticipations than the placid patter of normative paradox. Such is Seneca's denunciation of rhetoric and dialectic,[31] and, more remarkable, his recurrent attacks upon Stoic paradoxes themselves.[32] Despite his oft-repeated allusions to Stoicism as "our School," he is not innocent of posting an innuendo or cutting aspersion of Stoicism's venerable founding fathers, including even Zeno.[33] Furthermore, Seneca will at times sound, with ringing eloquence, the brazen note of independence from all philosophical systems, urging one's progress upon a private path: "For I have surrendered myself to no one; I bear no one's name. I heavily rely upon the judgment of great men, but I also claim something for my own" (*Ep.* 45.4; cf. *De Vita Beata* 3.2).

Not even the commonplace of the Stoic *sapiens* escapes questioning, for not only does Seneca repeatedly deny that he himself is a *sapiens*,[34] but he frequently treats the *sapiens* in such a way as to suggest that perhaps there is *none at all*: "Do you know what sort of man I term 'the good man' (*vir bonus*)? . . . he, like the phoenix, appears perhaps once every five hundred years."[35] All of us humans are, after all, Seneca tells us, fools—*dementissimi* (*Ep.* 70.3); all men have sinned—*peccavimus omnes* (*De Clem.* 1.6.3); and thereafter he informs us that even the *sapiens* must pass through error in order to achieve "innocence" (*De Clem.* 1.6.4).

In a kindred strain Seneca informs his friend Serenus that one of the solemn "rules" for securing tranquillity of mind is—frenzy. "[The mind] *must* revolt from the customary, must be savagely carried away, champing at the bit, sweeping its rider along, and mounting to a height it would have feared to approach on its own" (*De Tranq. An.* 17.11). That the seemingly staid Stoic philosopher can recommend inspired madness as vehicle to rational calm appears most surprising. Yet such flagrant assertions dramatize for us a salient feature of Seneca's thought not often enough accentuated: his personal paradoxicality, his playfulness and wit.

Indeed many conventional scholars look upon Seneca as the sententious and ordinary Stoic philosopher, one who recites standard precepts and consolations. To such scholars, Seneca's distinctive quality may be his ability as a rhetorician. Moreover, some critics (fledglings in psychoanalysis) regard his prose as incoherent and without architectural control. For such critics, Seneca's writing is not merely trifling and conventional, but it also exposes a tissue of inconsistencies and contradictions so considerable that it is concluded that he is neurotic or even quite insane.[36]

I concede at once that Seneca's writings frequently reveal inconsistencies and contradictions, that his prose surely evidences the traditional motifs of the philosopher, the courtier, and the orator. Yet I should have to insist that many contradictions in his prose are best explained, not by the rhetorician's manual or the psychiatrist's couch, but by the muse's art. Seneca is clearly artist as well as philosopher, and my purpose here is to explore the philosopher's witty, shocking, and ironic side. Perhaps we might best investigate the workings of Senecan wit by observing in detail his practice in a single work.

IV   *Epistle 56*

Curiously enough, we have Seneca's encouragement in this undertaking. After perusing the first thirty-two letters of the *Epistulae Morales*—all of them pointedly filled with snippets, maxims, and *sententiae* neatly lifted from other authors and quoted by dozens to his correspondent Lucilius[37]—the reader is abruptly brought up short in Epistle 33. There, in a striking reversal, Seneca denounces the very principle of snipping, herding, and quoting! Stoics, we are now informed, should not descend to lifting sayings and phrases out of context: "Therefore abandon that hope that you can acquire the taste of great men's wit in summaries and abbreviations; the whole work must be examined, must be pondered" (*Ep.* 33.5).[38] Thus Seneca—that Silver Latin author singularly renowned for his *sententiae*—debunks the *sententia;* he advises us, rather, to taste of the work in its entirety: "the author's genius is woven into every line—and nothing from that tapestry can be extracted without damaging the whole" (*Ep.* 33.5).[39] It might prove fruitful, therefore, to take Seneca at his word: to study Senecan artistry in single works, to scrutinize in each its "simplicity and unity."[40] Let us examine Epistle 56; its rich admixture of the serious and the comic promises to be rewarding.

Here, as in the other *Epistulae Morales,* Seneca seeks to "instruct" his younger friend Lucilius in his withdrawal from public life and in his cultivation of contemplative pursuits. "I both approve and rejoice that you study diligently and that, sacrificing all else, you attend to this one goal: to become, each day, a better man" (*Ep.* 5.1). Seneca, himself recently retired from political office under Nero, pursues this selfsame course. The ideal, for both Seneca and Lucilius, is to become the *sapiens,* and Seneca serves as physician, cheerleader, and friend to the younger man. Seen as one of the epistles ostensibly offering Lucilius encouragement and *consilium,* Epistle 56 is, comically, a fiasco. The letter is a tissue of Senecan contradiction, confession, and reversal. As an exemplary piece demonstrating how Seneca himself progresses toward the meaningful employment of *otium* (leisure) and achievement of Stoic *tranquillitas,* it is masterfully inept.

First we learn that the sage philosopher has retired—not to any Sabine Farm or Arcadian grove—but to densest urban Rome. He lives, in fact, above a bathhouse; and his privacy and peace are as insecure as they might have been at Trimalchio's *cena* or upon Troy's plain. His enumeration of the scuffle, grunt, and shout of weight-lifters, bathers, masseurs, hawkers, vendors, thieves, and lavatory minstrels is a study in blatant city noise that is almost unique.[41] What is more, Seneca describes this cacophony with painful alertness to the quantity and quality of *every sound.*

Therefore, it is a humorous and unexpected "reversal" when this philosopher suddenly, with a herculean oath, vows that this furor disturbs him *not in the least:* "By Hercules, I am no more concerned about such noise than I am about ocean waves or splashing water . . ." (*Ep.* 56.3). Astonishingly, he has, he tells Lucilius, accustomed himself to such noise (*Sed iam me sic ad omnia ista duravi . . ., Ep.* 56.5). Then growing philosophical, he explains that the man at peace with himself cannot be violated by mere "externals." After all, the rational and pensive mind is capable, is it not, of achieving *vera tranquillitas?* Especially is this so when the mind in solitude is occupied with intellectual labor.

Well and good, we concede; the philosopher is displaying his control. But yet, even now, a ripple of disturbance is admitted to this calm; for paradoxically, although Seneca in passing notes that his retirement has been marked by an absolute renunciation of his civic and political inclinations, *it is not so;* for he confesses that "sometimes, in that hiding-place, where weariness and fear have cast me, my ambition breaks out again" (*Ep.* 56.9). A public zeal and aspiration still haunt the philosopher's breast! Where, then, is that *vera tranquillitas* that had but lately abolished all that metropolitan clamor? However, Seneca continues so smoothly and quietly to analyze the recurrence—in others—of *mala mentis humanae* that one is induced to believe that his fleeting admission of fault in himself had been but a *lapsus calami* and nothing more. But this is not the case: again Seneca admits that he has not accomplished a Stoic retirement: *Otiosi videmur, et non sumus* ("We seem to be in retirement, yet are not," *Ep.* 56.11). Patently, Seneca is nothing akin to the Stoic *sapiens;* but this does not prevent him from continuing in a strain of moral exhortation, his rhetoric rising steadily to a climax, praising to Lucilius the virtues of the Stoic wise man—tranquillity, constancy, duty, control.

Approaching now the apex of his theme, the orator above the bathhouse, disquieted himself and yet extolling quiescence, enunciates sacred lines from Vergil: "And I, who used to be unruffled by flying spears or Greeks surrounding me in hostile bands, am now terrified by every breeze; in my anxiety, every sound arouses me, fearing equally for my companion and the burden on my back."[42] This is the Vergilian text he intones, partitions, and expounds. Yet, somehow, it strikes the reader as a curiously inappropriate selection for a peroration celebrating serenity and calm. It is strangely backward; for, from the Stoic point of view, the fearless Aeneas of the first two lines is the pattern of the *sapiens* (*Prior ille sapiens est,* Seneca tells Lucilius), fearless and staunch, deaf even to the noise of battle. But in the pair of succeeding lines, as if by some garish falling-off, the *sapiens* disappears, and there the suddenly human and fearful Aeneas stands upon the field, bearing the responsibilities of family and state, leading Ascanius by the hand and sustaining Anchises upon his back. Placidly, Seneca compares this dutiful Aeneas with luxurious men, those incapable of achieving Stoic wisdom or of ever transcending the lowly pleasures of the materialistic world.

Surely we are ill at ease with the analogy: the legendary founding father's moral stance in relation to his family seems right,[43]
but Seneca's associating Aeneas with cowardice and self-concern
appears to us perverse. Yet Seneca evades this issue, proceeding to
deliver his final point: Lucilius will know that he has obtained
the status of *sapiens* when no clamor ruffles him or chases him
away. On that note, Seneca concludes his epideictic declamation.

The reader, however, is far from feeling a sense of fulfillment.
The contradictions we have noted between Seneca's practice and
his preachment, between the loopholes in his argument and the
suave assurance of his tone, are too disturbing. And Lucilius is
disturbed; immediately, as *adversarius*, he interjects: "But why
live in the midst of such noise? Why not escape from it?" And, in
a trice, in what is the most striking reversal of the whole epistle,
Seneca totally capitulates: "You're right. I'll move away." He had,
he owns to Lucilius, merely sought to "test" himself; but now,
like Odysseus, who had stopped his companions' ears with wax,
he will sail past the Sirens in safety! With such an assertion,
comparing his own capitulation to Odysseus' epical triumph,[44] the
letter ends.

The "test" that Seneca has administered to himself he has
failed; the noises he has sought to suppress, the ambition he
would stifle, the argument he has constructed—all his intentions
are vanquished. What are we to make of this Seneca, whose
lecture to Lucilius upon privacy and endurance concludes with
agitation and Sirens, whose epic analogies emanate from the
bathhouse, whose "testing" of himself he flunks?

V   *The Harmony of Wisdom and Wit*

There can be no mistake about it; in this epistle, as elsewhere,
Seneca's artistry in paradox is clearly evident: the succession of
witty reversals, the turns of the argument, the dramatic agitations
concluding in *eversiones* (overturnings) are the witnesses to form,
mastered by the *artifex* and craftsman. But what, for the philosopher, is such artistry's purpose? How can moral earnestness with-
stand, let alone be enforced by, the posturings and pranks of
play? There should be little doubt that this philosopher's jocu-
larity and art are meaningful. For Seneca's jesting play is, uti-
mately, like that of Diogenes, of Horace, or of Plato, deeply in
earnest. Indeed, ethical earnestness cannot reasonably thrive in

an atmosphere of gloomy solemnity or of tedious self-righteous-
ness. Rather, as the Earl of Shaftesbury once argued, moral truth
urgently needs the support of wit.[45] By supplying such support,
Seneca manages to coalesce traditional Stoic teaching with a
sensitive urbanity.

Herodotus records that the Egyptian Pharaoh Amasis was
severely criticized by so-called public-spirited citizens for his
custom of devoting his mornings to affairs of state, but his after-
noons to convivial levity. Amasis had replied to them: "Archers,
when they wish to use them, string their bows; but when done,
unstring the bows. For if always kept strung, they would break,
and so, when needed, be useless. So too is man's condition:
should he always be serious and forbid himself some share of
[relaxation and] play, he would unawares suffer a stroke or run
mad. Knowing this, I apportion part of my time to each—to
seriousness and to play."[46] And so it is with Seneca; in one epistle,
he tells Lucilius: "just as the engraver relaxes his overstrained
and weary eyes, and calls them away from their work—'taking
a holiday,' as the saying goes—so we from time to time should
relax our mind and revive it with amusements" (*Ep.* 58.25). For
even the Stoic sage requires the saturnalia of the mind, what
Wallace Stevens has termed "One's grand flights, one's Sunday
baths, / One's tootings at the weddings of the soul. . . ."[47] In
like manner, Seneca would argue that no man is wise unless
capable of playfulness and folly. For the man who sustains but
one side is flat. Whereas, to be well rounded, every man must,
even at the outset of his journey toward wisdom, recognize both
his capacity for virtue as well as his propensity to folly. Every
apprentice to wisdom and justice must, like the Stoic hero
Hercules, travel a course, undertake labors, confront even madness. Seneca is fully aware that upon such a journey every argument, every "turn," every paradox, and every precept serves the
selfsame goal—to "exercise" and to "sharpen" the mind (*Ep.*
124.21.)

Thus, the two sides of Senecan practice are essential: wisdom
and folly, *ratio* and *ludus*, the taut bow and the bow unstrung.
Both of these serve man upon his Herculean quest. For Seneca is
not completely the fool: he lucidly perceives that, in man, reason
dictates the aspiration to wisdom, just as human folly undermines
that quest. So in the case of the man who struggles and aspires,

Seneca understands: "He will not have a level journey; he must encounter ups and downs, be tossed about, and guide his ship in troubled waters" (*De Prov.* 5.9). And Seneca cites with approbation the ambition of Phaëthon—despite the fact that Phaëthon, like Bellerophon and Icarus, is traditionally associated with vain, proud, and even foolish aspiration: "The road is pleasing, Phaëthon says; I shall ascend. To travel such a route is worth the effort, even though I fall" (*De Prov.* 5.11).[48]

Such is the heart of Senecan irony: like Amasis, he knew the straight path and the upward climb, but he also knew the byways and the pleasures of turning aside. Moreover, like Phaëthon, he realized the pitfalls, entanglements, and jolts encountered in life's difficult journey. What is remarkable concerning his ironic double view is his zeal to acknowledge and to harmonize the discordant parts of his philosophic song: "I want my mind to be of such quality: let it possess many arts, many precepts, *exempla* drawn from many ages; but let all be harmonized into one" (*Ep.* 84.10).

CHAPTER 6

Form and Art

TOO seldom is it recognized that Seneca in his prose is artist as well as philosopher, that his writings display a mixture of seriousness, wit, and art woven together into significant form. Such artistry is perhaps most readily observable on the verbal level, by examining sentences, words, and phrases. Thus, if Seneca has not been acknowledged a significant artist in the shaping of completed works, he has at least been recognized as a striking stylist and master of word and phrase.

I *Seneca's Style*

We are at first impressed by his brevity, his capacity to strike off terse, almost stichomythic sentences, aptly framed.

Damus nos aurae ferendos. Expavescimus dubia pro certis. Non servamus modum rerum. Statim in timorem vertit scrupulus. (*Ep.* 13.13–14) (We are the sport of the winds;[1] we tremble at what is dubious as though it were certain. We do not retain a sense of proportion. The smallest concern immediately converts us to panic.)

And Seneca very frequently transforms this trenchant, clipped utterance into striking maxims:

Multis timendi attulit causas timeri posse. (*Ep.* 14.10) (Many a man who inspires fear is himself subject to fear.)

Viam eunti aliquid extremum est; error immensus est. (*Ep.* 16.9) (For one travelling a route there is some end; but straying is endless.)

Maximum negotium tecum habes; tu tibi molestus es. (*Ep.* 21.1) (You are your own worst enemy; you annoy yourself.)

Infirmi animi est pati non posse divitias. (*Ep.* 5.6)
(The weak mind cannot endure wealth.)

It is this quality in him, the repeated creation of *sententiae,* that
has been most often remarked about his style.[2] It is certainly true,
as has been frequently observed, that Seneca is far from being the
first to develop the curt, clipped, epigrammatic style.[3] Others, too,
had tended to foster a terseness and point, the *style coupé,* that
is at the opposite extreme from the long, stately, and measured
periods of Ciceronian eloquence. Yet it should be noted that
Seneca is the master in this kind of writing, the first major
philosopher to write with such wit, precision, and sparkling con-
ciseness.

There are additional features of Senecan performance that
deserve recognition. In the following passage, Seneca warns
against the ostentatious philosophers who parade their unique-
ness, pretending either a pious poverty or a worldly wealth:

Non splendeat toga, ne sordeat quidem. Non habeamus argentum, in
quod solidi auri caelatura descenderit, sed non putemus frugalitatis in-
dicium auro argentoque caruisse. Id agamus, ut meliorem vitam se-
quamur quam vulgus, non ut contrariam; alioquin quos emendari
volumus, fugamus a nobis et avertimus. Illud quoque efficimus, ut nihil
imitari velint nostri, dum timent, ne imitanda sint omnia. (*Ep.* 5.3)
(Let the toga be neither splendid nor sordid. Let's not possess silver
inlaid with gold, but neither let us think it frugality to do without gold
and silver. We should seek to lead a life not opposed to, but better
than the masses; otherwise, we repel those whom we wish to improve.
We likewise cause them to want to imitate us in nothing while they
fear that they must imitate us in everything.)

The short, rhythmic balance of Seneca's pointed prose lends itself well indeed to the argument in this selection, which calls for
sanity, "balance," the Aristotelian "mean." Moreover, Seneca adds
much to enrich the texture of his prose. The juxtapositioning, in
the first line, of *splendeat* with *sordeat* introduces antithesis and
alliteration,[4] and in the reproduction of like sounds at the ends of
words toward the close—*volumus, fugamus . . . avertimus . . .
efficimus*—Seneca employs *homeoteleuton.*

In addition, Seneca's prose is relaxed, forthright, conversational;
one letter opens:

Sic est, non muto sententiam: fuge multitudinem, fuge paucitatem, fuge etiam unum. Non habeo, cum quo te communicatum velim. (*Ep.* 10.1)[5]
(So it is; I don't change my mind: flee the crowd, flee small groups, flee even a single person! I don't want to share you with anyone.)

The very repetition of *fuge* introduces *anaphora* and incremental balancing, features common in his writing. Even more importantly, the second sentence introduces a witty "turn" in the thought: Seneca wants Lucilius to withdraw in total solitude—only that Seneca might have him! Such turns, such unexpected reversals, utilizing *paraprosdokeon*, are quite common.

Satis ipsum nomen philosophiae, etiam si modeste tractetur, invidiosum est. . . . (*Ep.* 5.2)
(The very name of philosophy, even when modestly pursued, is invidious enough.)

Here a sentence beginning with *satis,* "enough," concludes, unexpectedly, with *invidiosum,* "invidious."

Together with such terse, unexpected development, Seneca frequently adds an easy, ironic colloquialism. In one epistle, for example, he reports the spectators' depravity at the gladiatorial shows. Even during the interludes, they call for bloodthirsty amusement:

Intermissum est spectaculum: "interim iugulentur homines, ne nihil agatur." (*Ep.* 7.5)
(There's an intermission: "Nothing's going on: cut some more throats to pass the time.")

Thus, Seneca supplies his succinct style with textural richness, chatty precision, and incisive sarcasm. And precisely these traits serve to make his epistles—and his philosophy—vigorous and quick. He may complain otherwise:

Modo dicebam tibi, in conspectu esse me senectutis; iam vereor, ne senectutem post me reliquerim. (*Ep.* 26.1)
(I was just telling you, that I was approaching old age; I now fear that I've left old age behind!)

But the graceful and intense verve of Senecan prose artistry suggests that its author is very, very much alive.[6]

II *Art in the* De Providentia

Seneca's artistic prose may be observed, of course, not merely at the sentence level, but in complete, individual works as well. It will prove worthwhile to examine a work like the *De Providentia,* one of the philosophical prose treatises, to discern in it, what is too seldom observed—an ample and deliberately artful formal control. If the *De Providentia* is not the best of the *Dialogi,* yet it is one of the shortest and surely one of the most polished and clear; it may serve as a useful exemplar of Senecan practice.

On the surface, however, we might be more inclined to think of a piece like the *De Providentia* as a declamation, or formal argument; *oratio,* Seneca terms it (*De Prov.* 3.1),[7] that is, "speech." As such, it is rigorously organized. Resolved: "Why, with a Providence existing, misfortunes in some way happen to good men." Taking the affirmative side of the argument, Seneca must make it his business to develop a *confirmatio,* a defense of Providence and of misfortune.

And he does so with rhetorical skill, with a keen sense for the disposition of the parts of his agreement. First, with a *praeteritio,* he observes at length to Lucilius that it is unnecessary to demonstrate that there *is* a Providence, that is, an eternal law and eternal order; whatever appears to be accidental or blind and disorderly is, in fact, predetermined in precise, measurable degrees, like the tides that are regulated by the moon (*De Prov.* 1.1-3).

Indeed, man is God's friend, student, similitude, and even progeny. Like a strict father, God trains and hardens his pupils, and there is no question of evil befalling the good man. Adversity is absolutely necessary for the education of the mind, as it is in the training of the bodies of athletes. As a father, God wishes to admire the dexterity and endurance of his athletes. And the contest, worthy of God's presence as spectator, is the good man's struggle with misfortune. Here, Cato the Younger is produced as the perfect illustration of the successful contestant in a mortal battle (*De Prov.* 2.9-12).

The reference to the patriotic Cato leads Seneca to a stronger assertion: that misfortunes are only seemingly so, that they are in fact strokes of good fortune when they beset the good man, and that, above all, adversity indeed serves the good of all humanity.

Loss of family, ill health, exile, death: all these are "good" for the virtuous man. The philosopher Demetrius is cited as an authority on this text, and thereafter Seneca produces a team of exemplars: Mucius, Fabricius, Rutilius, Regulus, Socrates, and Cato. All suffered greater and greater hardships—from poverty and personal pain to death itself (*De Prov.* 3.4-14).

The suffering, with forbearance and self-control, even of that last extremity, death, is the sign, Seneca urges at the outset of 4.1, of *magnus vir,* the great man. Such affliction, paradoxically, establishes the great man, is his badge and credentials. Thus, Seneca goes so far as to urge that adversity literally brings "joy" (*gaudium*) to the man aspiring to virtue. God is, seen in this context, merely granting "favors" to men when he introduces them to suffering. It is a mark of his love.

Seneca has clearly turned the argument to his own advantage and developed it with vigor. First, misfortunes are *not* misfortunes; they are the virtuous man's boon. And secondly, far from "permitting" misfortunes to occur, God actually perpetrates them out of respect and even love! The argument has clearly been developed in terms of paradoxes, progressing in an unexpected vein, and it is likewise progressing climactically. Thus, roused by this time to speaking heatedly, the philosopher presses his precepts with greater emotion: "Flee pleasure, flee enervating good fortune, which drown the soul and, unless something intervenes to alert men to human destiny, they continue lethargic, as if in perpetual drunkenness" (*De Prov.* 4.9). Indeed, having scored this point, he can now insist that so-called good fortune is positively dreadful: "While whatever has exceeded due measure is harmful, the most dangerous excess is unbridled happiness" (*De Prov.* 4.10). Lucilius himself is implicitly cited, now, as an example of the impoverished man who has been hardened and become successful by his training, his diligence, and familiarity with labor (*De Prov.* 4.13).

Moreover, in *De Prov.* 5.1, recurring to the earlier assertion (*De Prov.* 3.1), Seneca can urge that when the best men offer themselves up to adversity, it is for the good of all men. The best men must serve in the senate, as in the army, or a nation is lost. Virtuous men, fortunately, are willing and volunteer. And here Seneca propounds what is thus far his most important point: the *vir bonus* presents himself to fate and to fortune of his own free will (*De Prov.* 5.6). Here, there is an allusion to the Stoic founders, Zeno and Chrysippus. They had maintained that man is like a dog tied behind a cart: if he does not walk with the wagon, he will be dragged along.[8] Seneca, with this maxim obviously in mind, observes that "Good men are not dragged by fortune, they follow her and keep pace with her steps. Had they known how, they would have passed her" (*De Prov.* 5.4). Demetrius again is quoted, this time at length, stressing the importance of the good man's voluntary consent to the operations of fate and the gods.

In mounting toward the argument's climax, Seneca had made his most telling proposal heretofore, asserting man's voluntariness. He now enters upon the high-water-mark of his case: man *must* submit to fate. And this is the crucial point of the argument, since it strikingly refutes the language in which, at the outset, the very controversy was framed. There, it had been asked why misfortunes "happen to" or "fall to" (*accido*) the good man. Clearly, such a verb denoted *accident* or *chance*. Here it is asserted plainly that not fitful haphazard governs earthly affairs, but rather necessity (*necessitas*); an irrevocable course (*irrevocabilis cursus*) (*De Prov.* 5.8), like the tides mentioned at the outset, flows through all the universe. And not merely is man alone committed to this stream—God himself must adhere to the natural laws circumscribing this river.[9]

Thus the *sapiens* or *vir bonus* is elevated to a level with God; both must run with the rolling cart—or even attempt to surpass it. Consequently, because he is godlike, the wise man functions as, literally, a representative of God and a teacher of men: "Why do good men suffer certain afflictions? That they may teach others to endure them; they were born to be exemplars" (*De Prov.* 6.3).

In a well-timed peroration, God himself speaks the concluding lines of the dialogue: indeed, man has a volitional capacity that even surpasses that of myself; he is able to elect to live—and to die. Man, unlike God, is capable of outstripping that cart: he may elect what is the ultimate decision-making, to end his life, to transcend his suffering by suffering itself" (*De Prov.* 6.3-9). By a cunning development in the argument, Seneca, who had commenced by defending the gods, concludes with God's defense of man. And the emphasis is squarely upon Stoic matter—the rational choice and election available to man.

As a result, Seneca's *De Providentia* is no mere schoolboy's rehearsal of the traditional lines of oratory and argument. The commonplace *exordium, narratio, argumentatio,* and *peroratio*[10] of the rhetorical schools is not simply reproduced with abject mimicry. The development of an inspired and heated argument to a climax is unusual; and the recital of the peroration by God himself is unique. Moreover, as we have observed, Seneca's *De Providentia* is artfully constructed; what he urges as the necessary and meaningful organization of the universe can well be applied to his own literary creation: "Cause depends upon cause, . . . affairs are controlled by a long series of events" (*De Prov.* 5.7). His argument is boldly and distinctly posited and developed.

But there is another feature of *De Providentia's* artistry that must be perceived before we have done with Seneca's deployment of form—the dramatic qualities so significantly a feature of the dialogue.[11] Throughout the *De Providenia* are to be discerned personal allusions that render the debate intimate and particular. We have already observed the allusion to Lucilius (*De Prov.* 4.13-14), who had labored mightily to advance his social standing until he had become a member of the equestrian class and a procurator of Sicily. There are further allusions to Seneca himself. The interlocutor asks Seneca if it is for the good of men that they be exiled, lose their wealth, witness the death of wife or children, and endure bad health and public ignominy (*De Prov.* 3.2). Surely all of these trials and tribulations had been suffered by the philosopher himself in the reign of Claudius! Again, further on, a new voice seems almost to be speaking to Seneca alone: How can one ever know how you will endure poverty, if you luxuriate merely in riches? How will you be able to confront infamy and popular hatred if you only experience public applause? How will you sustain the loss of children, the advent of old age? "I listened to you when you were giving consolation to others: had you been consoling yourself, had you forbidden yourself to grieve, then I would have admired you" (*De Prov.* 4.5).[12] Implicit here is the calling-to-account of the philosophical writer of *consolationes,* Seneca himself. It need hardly be observed that such private innuendo and reference only serve to surcharge the

argument with an interest and a friction that an aloof discourse
would never attain.[13]

Most dramatic, however, of Seneca's practices in the *De
Providentia* is his elaboration of the conflict or *agon* between a
hypothetical Lucilius and the philosopher in this dialogue. As
interlocutor or *adversarius* throughout the piece, the hypothetical
Lucilius implements the sense of drama considerably and enhances this work's fictional art. As the original questioner (in this
imaginary dramatic debate, a device that rhetoricians term *ser-
mocinatio*), this ostensible Lucilius is portrayed as repeatedly
raising objections (with an *inquis*) to the course and development
of the argument. Having originally inquired why, despite the
presence of Providence in the universe, many evils fall to the lot
of good men, this supposed Lucilius is remarkable for his intran-
sigence. He continues, throughout, to pose questions.[14] And,
amazingly, his question is ever the same! Even near the very
end of the discourse, renouncing all of the development and
progress within this essay, this dramatic opponent has progressed
not in the least. But why, he asks at the close (as he has throughout), does evil sometimes fall to *viri boni?* For sheer density, this
adversary is almost unexcelled; he simply has not followed the
course and growth of the argument!

And his fictional obtuseness, as a dominant feature of the artistic creation, necessitates the very climactic conclusion of the
quarrel. Utilizing an obvious instance of *deus ex machina*, Seneca
at the close of the *De Providentia* introduces God himself. Lucilius, like Job, has simply been too dull to follow the line of the
argument. Only God, it is implied, can placate and intervene,
and so permit the *dénouement*. Consequently, at the climax of the
De Providentia, it is to the imagined Lucilius that God must
speak. And God's closing words are, after the manner of Euripides, suitable to the occasion. Because of this Lucilius' hard-
headedness, the deity speaks, despite the exaltation of the subject
matter, with a caustic and disruptive levity. Can you find no easy
path to goodness? the God declaims: what a pity! Yet (and his
voice is filled with an almost sardonic irony), I have created man
such a meager thing, so easily situated upon an inclined plane,
that he can facilely tumble into nonbeing. How easy, this God
almost jeers, it is for man to depart from his little stage. The
tiniest penknife opens the portals of the other world! Are you not

ashamed at a test so easy? Aren't you ashamed to fear what may be accomplished by the littlest stroke?[15]

Here the argument comes to a close. Seneca has managed to complicate and to enrich what could have been simply formal argument or facile debate. It is no wonder that such a piece is designated *dialogue*. For the contention of voices calling for ennobling deeds and the hesitant quaver of the vacillating *adversarius* manage to strike just the right note of realism. Seldom does philosophy so readily—or so handily—achieve the texture of tense physical reality. Seneca recognizes that mere discourse, here, is not enough. He renders his dramatic presentation far more believable by creating an *adversarius* who constantly demurs and a deity who ruthlessly wields an incisive rebuttal. Certainly, it was a brilliant stroke to have given, in this dialogue, the last word about man's fate to the deity himself. Seneca's success in this work lies precisely in his fostering the drama of irony, contention, and disbelief. His theater, because of the waywardness of the actors, is quite full and complete.

III   *Seneca's Dramatic Art:* Epistle 53

If Seneca's dramatic art is evident in the *De Providentia*, it is even more distinctly successful in groups of the *Epistulae Morales* and especially in individual letters. For Seneca's polished prose has achieved in this major work, the *Letters to Lucilius*, the pinnacle of effectiveness and control.

Yet in spite of Seneca's achievement, critics of the *Epistulae Morales ad Lucilium* have too often been inclined to treat Seneca's letters too literally, and particularly is this the case with *Epistles* 49–57. In dealing with these nine epistles, scholars have repeatedly fallen into a meticulous preoccupation with geography and chronology: *When* was Seneca at Puteoli? *How often* did he visit Naples? *Whence* the repeated trips in and out of Baiae?[16] If these letters be viewed thus superficially, one would merely perceive in them the representation of an aged Seneca, discarded from court, discredited with Nero, and in fear of his life, posting and hobbling ineptly among the luxurious resorts in Campania.

In contrast to such a view, we should like to propose that Letters 49–57 are coherent and meaningful, not geographically or chronologically, but thematically. Unlike the immediately preceding letters, 40–48, which are directed outward to Lucilius—

responding to Lucilius' own book (46), warning Lucilius about melodramatic, fast-talking philosophers (40), exhorting him to avoid sophistic argumentation and vain syllogistic logic (45, 48) —the letters that follow are abruptly, personally concerned with Seneca himself. In sharp contrast to those earlier epistles which gave general advice (recommending the humane treatment of slaves, since all men are alike, 47; or abstractly extolling self-reliance and the virtues of leading one's life according to nature and reason, 41), we are suddenly confronted with the concrete instance of Seneca himself.

For the most part, these later epistles (49–57) are concerned with the busy, futile traveler. A dominant chord is recurringly struck about such a scurrying, affected traveler: Seneca cites with approval Socrates' retort to the man complaining he has not profited from traveling, "You got what you deserved; you were traveling in your own company." For Seneca emphatically censures such tourism—especially in himself. "What's the use of crossing the sea and going from city to city? If you want to escape your difficulties, you must not change your residence, but your character. Suppose you have come to Athens or Rhodes or any other city. What difference does it make what character it has? You will be bringing your own to it" (*Ep.* 104.7–8). Present also in most of these epistles is a strong melodic line devoted to *meditatio mortis*. One must ever think upon death,[17] reflecting that "a whole lifetime is hardly sufficient to learn this single fact —scorn of life" (*Ep.* 111.5). For death is every man's lot: "You will die, not because you are sick, but because you are living" (*Ep.* 78.6).

Moreover, these themes—of vain traveling and of impending death—are noteworthy precisely because they are themes suddenly and intimately dramatized; it is the aging Seneca himself who is the substance of the argument. Thus, *Epistle* 49 introduces the personal setting: Seneca, the sentimental traveler, has returned to Campania and, becoming engrossed in fond memories, poignantly comes to recognize the rapid passing of *his* time: "death is pursuing me, life is fleeing from me" (*Ep.* 49.9). Seneca himself is confronted with the prospect of his own life and his own death, and *Epistle* 50 reinforces this theme by allusion to his wife's *fatua*, Harpasté, observing that all men are, in a sense, benighted *fatui*; and he concludes this epistle by speaking particularly of his own folly, his own medicine and sickness. *Epistles* 51, 53, 54, 55, 56, 57 then produce very concrete instances of Seneca the *fatuus* and aged traveler who makes specific local journeys in and about Baiae, Cumae, and Naples. He himself is the effete traveler and object of *meditatio mortis.*

These are the constant themes in *Epistles* 49–57, themes juxtaposed, merging, harmoniously made to blend. Yet such themes are united, not by the canons of history or autobiography, but by the mastery of art. As exemplar of such esthetic order, we shall here examine *Epistle* 53.

Seneca frequently was fond of insisting that he himself was no *sapiens.*[18] On the contrary, as we have indicated, his assertion in *Epistle* 50 establishes the tone for the letters immediately to follow: all men are in some degree corrupt; "no one acquires a good mind without having experienced evil. . . ." (*Ep.* 50.7). And such acquisition of evil is assuredly to be observed of Seneca the *fatuus,* the fool: "if at any time I want to be amused by a fool, I don't have to look far: I laugh at myself" (*Ep.* 50.2).[19] Accordingly, the epistles immediately following appear to go out of their way to present Seneca as a ludicrous fool. "Ordinarily, we are reluctant to accept the conventional pose of the satirist: the self-appointed censor who seems to delight in telling us, derisively, of our sins. But it is a measure of the greatest satirists (perhaps the greatest men) that they recognize their own involvement in the folly of human life and willingly see themselves as victims, in obscure ways, of their own art."[20] Perhaps nowhere in the *Epistulae Morales* does Seneca appear more of the clown than in *Epistle* 53.

In this letter, the aging philosopher has attempted to make the short sea voyage across the bay from Puteoli to Naples. As might be expected—in tragedy, or in farce!—when he is in his trip precisely midway across, there is a "sea-change," the weather suffers *peripeteia:* a storm breaks and rough sea commences. The aged and sage philosopher instantly panics and demands to be put ashore. Overcome with mundane and indecorous seasickness and vomiting, Seneca in a consternation passionately insists that his pilot draw near the shore. And, without further ado, while the boat is still some distance from the shore, the philosopher, mantle and all, plops into icy waters and wallows dizzily ashore.

Nor are his difficulties yet at an end. For, still seasick and aghast, the philosopher must contend with the land. In another reversal, it is now the shore that offers opposition: "I understood that there's every good reason why sailors fear the land" (*Ep.* 53.4). Surprisingly, the land too is unkind! Seneca struggles ridiculously to clamber up the rocks, seeking in his haste to strike his own "path," not merely over, but *through,* the rocks: "can you imagine what I suffered while I crawled through the rocks, seeking a path, or making one?" (*Ep.* 53.4).

Up to this point, Seneca's debasement has been considerable. It is made yet more telling by a number of mock-heroic allusions. Referring to the orderly fashion in which ships are settled at anchor, their bows facing seaward,[21] the philosopher wryly notes that he does no such thing: there is no time, and he abandons ship! Later, he compares himself, with handsome ineptitude, to Odysseus. Indeed, upon this occasion he reaches the lowest level in his descent, for with this analogy his reasoning has become corrupt as well as his courage, and he rationalizes, with dreadful illogic propounding the thesis that Odysseus was shipwrecked so often because he suffered (like Seneca himself) marine nausea! "Know this: Ulysses was not fated from birth to suffer shipwreck everywhere because of an angry sea: he was merely a victim of sea-sickness!" (*Ep.* 53.4). Achieving the low point of unbecoming timorousness—like Horace just cast ashore from the dangerous "waters" of his tempestuous mistress, Pyrrha[22]—Seneca vows to go to sea no more.

From this depth in the recounted action, the epistle suddenly takes a new "turn," commencing now a course of reflection and meditation. After a rubdown, he begins to consider "how much we forget our own infirmities, even physical ones" (*Ep.* 53.5). This might be true, but the reader is hardly prepared to consider sea-sickness a *vitium*—a "fault" or "vice." Moreover, the case is strained: once a man has been seasick, he is hardly likely to "forget" his "difficulty," and absently wander out upon the ocean upon occasion! Furthermore, the argument built upon this "thesis" is lumpishly farfetched: a man will not remember he has the gout, Seneca explains, but when his illness mounts, when pain becomes excruciating, when his foot swells and his ankle distends horribly, the victim then will "notice" his illness! He certainly does!

But this self-evident piece of seriousness has been constructed only to prepare for a reversal, a turning in 53.7 to the real point:

although physical illness as it increases becomes noticeable, the opposite is true of moral disease. The more corrupt the mind, the less one is aware of corruption. With this "turn," the authentic subject of the epistle emerges: spiritual disease, moral turpitude. He who is deeply asleep is oblivious; likewise, he who is engrossed in vice. "Why does no one admit his faults?" *(Ep.* 53.8). Because the patient is unaware of his disease.

Now Seneca, having arrived upon the proper track at last, mounts his resolution, delivered in the tones of a peroration: awaken from slumber; arise from the disease; turn to *philosophia.* "Philosophy alone will rouse us, she alone will shake off our heavy slumber: devote yourself wholly to her" *(Ep.* 53.8). We observe that, curiously, the epistle has moved from Seneca's own physical weakness to "our" diseases, only then to conclude with an exhortation to "you," Lucilius. However, the shiftings and turnings that we have remarked all appear to have been swept away by the energy and moral zeal of this concluding appeal to *philosophia.*

But the epistle does not end here. Instead, it continues to expound the vision of Philosophia as heroine, slowly pushing the argument to its extremity. First, Philosophy is understood as a lover, perhaps one even to be taken in marriage: "You are worthy of her, she is worthy of you: embrace one another" *(Ep.* 53.8). Soon the imagery changes, and she is seen as a haughty mistress, perhaps an aristocratic princess: "Philosophy exercises her own dominion; she is not the receiver but the giver of time; she is not for one's spare time, she demands regularity; she is mistress" *(Ep.* 53.9). She appears somewhat of an overlord, a dominating and dictatorial power—almost masculine. And, sure enough, in the next figure, her potency is compared with Alexander's power when he invaded Asia: she will seize all, merely conferring an occasional privilege upon her thralls. In the figure immediately following, she has become a deity, the suppliant sitting at her side with devotion *(asside)* and worshiping *(cole)* her: "Turn your whole mind to her, sit beside her, worship her . . ." *(Ep.* 53.11). By such a progressive series of exalting metamorphoses, Philosophia has naturally transported the devotee a great distance: "you will far surpass all men, the gods will not far surpass you" *(Ep.* 53.11). That lowly follower, the slave, the vestal to Philosophy, is now rendered all but equal to the gods himself. And in a remarkable final step, he exceeds the gods! "There is one thing in which the *sapiens* surpasses God: God is without fear because of Nature's benefaction; the wise man, because of his own" (*Ep.* 53.11). By a double paradox, this slave to philosophy is suddenly emancipated, the servant manumitted, elevated, catapulted above the very gods. Then Seneca offers a last image of unexpected transformation: Philosophia, having been raised to godhood, abruptly descends to become—the warrior! She is immune to weapons hurled at her; spears cannot touch her. She paradoxically foils weapons by the mere *laxus sinus* (loose folds) of her robe. And in one final, threatening image, Philosophia becomes no longer defensive, but the warrior launching an attack: "some weapons she drives away, hurling them back upon the opponent" (*Ep.* 53.12). Here the letter ends.

Thus, an epistle that commenced ludicrously with disaster upon the water concludes with victory upon the battlefield; an epistle commencing with Seneca's physical defeat closes with Lucilius hypothetically exalted to spiritual triumph. It is all but impossible to trace precisely the argument's course, for the letter proceeds by leaps, by turns, by starts: it is no accident that in key places Seneca employs verbs like *excutio* (53.8) and *discutio* (53.12), emphasizing violent shaking and shattering.[23]

Of course, Seneca has always argued that life itself is the experience of jolts and stormy tossings: "What lies between our first and our last day is changeable and uncertain: if you judge it by its afflictions, life seems long even to a boy; if you judge it by its celerity, life seems short even to an old man. All things are slippery and false, more changeable than the weather; all things are hurled about and turn topsy-turvy at Fortune's command . . ." (*Ep.* 99.9). But we are likely to feel that his exaggerations in *Epistle* 53 have taken him too far. For if Seneca in the water is too laughably absurd at letter's outset, so also are *philosophia* and the *sapiens* too much elevated at the end. Obviously, *philosophia's* emergence in the closing moments as ominous champion, a Penthesilea or a Camilla, is paradoxically and logically unexpected; we do not anticipate the transcendent virtues of wisdom (exceeding even the gods') suddenly to descend to the battleground. It is unexpected—logically. But that is simply because this letter proceeds forcibly, disturbingly, wittily, not by the dissertations of logic, but by the fictions of art.

However, if the epistle be understood as a fiction, we observe that the letter's action unfolds with probability enough. First, the letter portrays the defeat, the satiric abasement of Seneca himself. From such a descent, the fictional "turning upwards" is common enough. Just after his marine disaster and defeat, and precisely in the middle of the letter, Seneca introduces the comparison of the flawed and vanquished man with the man immersed in deepest sleep (*Ep.* 53.7). Many a hero of epic and myth, we will recall, is at some low ebb in his journey subjected to just such a "sleep of prisoners," a slumber that has been termed by Edwin Honig a "regressive respite." "Just as sleep is traditionally equated with the will-less chaos of mind and matter before imagination and form have been imposed on it, so the dream [i.e., in "lighter sleep"], in turn, suggests the stirrings of intelligence toward wakefulness and order. Out of sleep the creative spirit, the light dividing the darkness, will move, having been fed and invigorated by rest."[24] Fictionally, the protagonist of this epistle must be emotionally debased, and fallen into a phase of somnolence, in order that he might, as Seneca points out, arise—*Expergiscamur ergo* (*Ep.* 53.8)—and turn to Philosophia. The course of this fictional journey is, in terms of suitable emotion and timing in its plot, quite right. For Seneca's *Epistle* 53 dramatizes the meditation of a man who rises from defeat to inspiring conquest.

In addition, there is one further pertinent employment of the letter's imagery which serves to unify and correlate the letter's parts. We have noted how this letter's imagery commenced in the ocean and concluded upon the plain. This is precisely the progress of imagery one often finds in heroic myth. Thus the Cumaean Sibyl forewarns Aeneas: "O, you who have experienced the vast dangers of the sea, still graver perils await you upon the land. . . ."[25] And she is exactly right: for half (Bks. I–VI) of the *Aeneid* deals with the perils of the sea, and the remaining half (Bks. VII–XII) with the toils of warfare upon the land. A similar bifurcation marks the *Odyssey,* twelve books being concerned with Odysseus' wanderings upon the sea, and twelve with his stamina and courage upon his native Ithacan soil. It is no accident that Seneca's epistle, echoing and alluding to both the *Odyssey* and the *Aeneid,* should similarly turn from the dangers of the sea to imagery of warfare and of victory upon the land.[26]

In epitome or in miniature, then, Seneca has successfully dramatized the central course and theme of a major heroic story: "By

Hercules, it is the mark of the great artist to have enclosed all in a little space" (*Ep.* 53.11). That should be achievement enough; but Seneca, more importantly, has done more, for he has scored the meaning of that heroic tour. Hence he informs us, toward the close of his letter: "What a great thing: to have man's infirmity and God's stability!" (*Ep.* 53.12). And it is so. What Seneca has dramatized and perceived is the route that must be taken in order to achieve such a goal. The imagined philosophic hero in such a piece must first "pass through" the imbecilities of manhood, before he can awaken and rise up to the quiescence and freedom of the gods. In *Epistle* 53, it is just such a fictive course that has been traveled and won.

IV   Epistle 57: A *Paradigm of Form*

Another epistle that may well serve as virtually a paradigm of Alexandrian form and art, accomplishing Callimachean fullness in a little space is *Epistle* 57. As a kind of counterpoint to the sea voyage of 53, *Ep.* 57 firmly fixes our landbound traveler—in the mud. Seneca on his journey to Naples is like Horace stumbling toward Brundisium (*Satire* I.5); the only "heroic" action encountered by the philosopher en route is the warlike contention of earth, both wet and dry. "We endured simultaneously two hardships diametrically opposed: on the same road, on the same day, we labored through mud and dust" (*Ep.* 57.2). Like the sturdy athlete, he is "anointed" with both: "after being anointed [with mud], we were sprinkled with sand in the Naples tunnel" (*Ep.* 57.1). Taking the short route, through the Naples tunnel, the philosopher is covered with dirt, choked with dust, immersed in blackness. Among other paradoxes, Seneca grimly observes that the feeble torches only serve to enhance the dark! [27]

Not only is the scene here, as so often, mock-epical, placing the philosopher in a silly plight while shedding on him a darkened light, but the letter is also replete with logical contradiction. For, despite the gloom, the battle, and the terrible dark, the philosopher (not courageous enough to venture upon another trip at sea) feels not the least fear (*sine metu*), but rather exuberance (*Ep.* 57.3). Yet immediately he confesses that, in speaking of such fearless alertness, he is *not* referring to himself: "I am not talking to you about myself, who am far from being acceptable, let alone perfect, but about a man over whom fortune has lost its power. . . ." Seneca in the tunnel is left behind, and we are traveling now with an ideal (and hypothetical) Stoic sage. In this digression, Seneca pauses to refute the traditional Stoic concept that the *sapiens* transcends emotion; on the contrary, Seneca surprisingly argues, the sage will blanch (*mutabitur color*) and shudder (*inhorrescet*); for he too is governed by emotions. Brave men may often, he explains, feel shock and revulsion, and even faint.[28] Shortly thereafter, Seneca is again refuting a general doctrine (that he terms "Stoical"), namely, that a man crushed beneath a great weight will have his soul fragmented and dispersed.[29]

Then, just as abruptly as Seneca had transferred his own journey in the tunnel to the shoulders of the courageous "wise man," he now reassumes the journey in his own person: he sees the light and emerges from the cave. From such an experience he is able to argue, in conclusion, that the soul is indeed everlasting and will ever emerge from the tomb of darkness into an immortal light.

Once again, the reader is confronted with an essay that begins on a trifling, antiheroic and comical note, but thereafter courses through alterations and contradictions, only to conclude in gravity and seriousness. What should impress us is precisely Seneca's ability to form such contraries into a unity, to weld a variety of tones into single-minded bliss. Most impressively, this multitude of ideas, this parcel of paradox and wit is unified by the dominant theme of journey, by the central fictional image of the darkling tunnel.

In terms of fictional progress, Seneca himself has entered the underground mine and pressed forward against gloomy obstacles, until he has again reached the light. Interestingly enough, such a descent into a cave is traditionally a mythic and religious experience, and Robert Turcan rightly observes of *Ep.* 57, "Seneca's souci de communiquer au lecteur quelque chose de l'ambiance religieuse . . . au spectacle des processions isiaques."[30] In actuality, myths of a *descensus ad inferos* appear in almost *every* mythology.[31] Innumerable deities (such as Attis, Osiris, Adonis, Persephone, Baal, Dionysus, Innana) endure the classic descent that, as an archetype of seasonal change, leads to subsequent rebirth, ascent, and return. Innumerable heroes, furthermore—Heracles, Aqhat, Orpheus, Cuchulain, Theseus, and later, Aeneas and Dante—reenact this selfsame journey.[32] Odysseus in the Homeric epic not only "descends" into the underworld in Book XI, but, as William

S. Anderson has shown, Odysseus' seven-year captivity on the isle
of Ogygia portrays residence in *another* land of the dead,[33] as do,
it may be similarly urged, his adventures among the Lotus-Eaters,
with Circe the enchantress, and in Polyphemus' cave. Odysseus
must literally harrow innumerable hells before he may return in
safety "home."

In every one of these cases, the entry into the cave or shady
grove is a necessity; death *must* be confronted (and endured) if
revivification is to follow. Thus Livy's Numa *must* consort with
Egeria in a dark grotto,[34] and Plato's neophytes *must* commence
life in the Cave[35] if they are ever to "transcend" it and rise "to see
the light." More recent legends of the Seven Sleepers and of Rip
Van Winkle remind us that a sleep must be endured, if the sleepers are to awaken. And Maynard Mack recalls that, in the eighteenth century, "The tradition of the Sage in a holy cave was in
any case widespread and so powerful that it persisted well into
the nineteenth century."[36]

The sun, too, in its daily setting and revival, was traditionally
conceived as traveling this selfsame infernal course, passing beneath the Western mountains, through a dark channel, to renewal
in the East—and to light.[37] Just such a solar and questing journey
is made by the Sumerian and Babylonian hero, Gilgamesh. Gilgamesh aspires, although a mortal, to discover Dilmun, Paradise,
"the garden of the sun," and to ask the ultimate questions "concerning the living and the dead." To do so, he must make the
incredible journey to the great mountain called Mashu, "which
guards the rising and the setting sun." Intrepidly, he enters the
dread gateway and

. . . followed the sun's road to his rising, through the mountain. When
he had gone one league the darkness became thick around him, for
there was no light, he could see nothing ahead and nothing behind him.
[And so for each of the next six leagues.] When he had gone eight
leagues Gilgamesh gave a great cry, for the darkness was thick and he
could see nothing ahead and nothing behind him. After nine leagues he
felt the north wind on his face, but the darkness was thick and there
was no light, he could see nothing ahead and nothing behind him.
After ten leagues the end was near. After eleven leagues the dawn light
appeared. At the end of twelve leagues the sun streamed out. [He was
in] the garden of the gods.[38]

Important, too, is our identification of such a night journey both with actual death and with the initiatory rites of the mystery cults that were devoted to apotheosized heroes: "when [the point of death] comes," Plutarch writes, of initiation rites,

> . . . [the soul] has an experience like that of men who are undergoing initiation into great mysteries; and so the verbs *teleutân* (die) and *te-leisthai* (be initiated), and the actions they denote, have a similarity. In the beginning there is straying and wandering, the weariness of running this way and that, and nervous journeys through darkness that reach no goal, and then immediately before the consummation every possible terror, shivering and trembling and sweating and amazement. But after this a marvelous light meets the wanderer, and open country and meadow lands welcome him; and in that place there are voices and dancing and the solemn majesty of sacred music and holy visions. And amidst these, he walks at large in new freedom, now perfect and fully initiated. . . .[39]

Seneca's artful *Epistle* 57 details, fictionally and in brief compass, just such a journey and initiation of the wise man. He has descended like the dead, "in crypta Neapolitana" (*Ep.* 57.1), and like the Orphic initiates, he has been bathed and immersed in mud.[40] Akin to visitants at the cave of Trophonius with their honey-cake, he has descended seeking self-knowledge and fulfillment—and has successfully re-emerged.[41] In miniature, as it were, Seneca has fully united myth with plot (*mythos*), fictionally creating and rehearsing a progress of the soul. The course of action within the epistle is exactly wedded to the process of his argument. For in both the action and the argument, he has descended into the crypt, been frightened and confounded, until ultimately suffering a "mutation" (*Ep.* 57.3, 6), until he and his epistle "have returned through a narrow opening" (*per exiguum foramen est reditus, Ep.* 57.8).

Seneca's own mental and physical journey in this letter, of course, portrays the struggles of a Stoic *proficiens* who wishes to become the *sapiens,* the experience of a man who sustains deadly fears until he arrives at a conviction of the soul's immortality. But Seneca's imaginative art consists in his utilizing imagery from the the great myths of *descensus* and from initiation rites in generating, as Plato had done before him, his plot. Despite his humor and his contradictions, and perhaps even because of them, his letter frames a coherent medallion precisely recounting the *sapiens'* initiation. As if approaching his *peripeteia* with a honey-cake, Seneca himself has struggled without sight, until at length his thought achieves the light.

It is Seneca's art that secures for him the measure of his success, and his carefully wrought imaginative creation that has conducted his argument, like the Orphic initiate, to a final joyous enlightenment. In the *De Vita Beata*, Seneca exactly summarizes his sense of such a spiritual journeying: "you must understand . . . that when we have exiled all that excites or terrifies us, continual tranquillity and freedom ensue; for when pleasures and fears have been eliminated, . . . boundless joy, unshaken and even-tempered, and peace and harmony of soul are experienced . . ." (*De Vita Beata* 3.4).

CHAPTER 7

Conclusion

SENECA'S continuous and insistent quest for tranquillity of soul was especially welcome to his contemporaries, who had witnessed the cruelties and tumult of the Neronian era. But to men of all centuries, Seneca's ardent zeal to enlighten the weary wanderer has had a most unusual appeal. With profound insight into human nature, he points out man's innate potential for constant moral progress—through reason. Hence, in his philosophic writings, Seneca depreciates abstract speculation and dialectic while he places a special emphasis upon ethics and moral instruction. In fact, *all* of his prose works—including his scientific studies—are ethical discourses, concerned with instructing his fellow men in the *ars vivendi*. As an eclectic philosopher, Seneca borrowed and amalgamated ideas from every school—the Stoic, the Cynic, the Epicurean, the Peripatetic, and the Academic. But his talent consisted not only in rendering such a diversity into a unity of his own but in expressing this synthesis in an original, terse, and striking style.

His dynamic thought and never-ending search for moral progress are dramatized repeatedly in *Dialogues* and *Letters* addressed to his friends, with whom he was most eager to share his possessions. Typically, he writes: "It is no pleasure to possess any good without a friend to share it" (*Ep.* 6.4; cf. *Ep.* 19.11). For to him, friendship, a rarity in every age (*De Benef.* 6.33.3), produces between men a partnership in all their interests (*Ep.* 3.2; 48.2–3; *De Benef.* 7.4.1; 7.12.1). Such friendship is sought even by the self-sufficient Stoic *sapiens* (*Ep.* 9.5).

Since Seneca addresses friends (and all mankind as would-be friends), he frequently uses a chatty, urbane, conversational style (*Ep.* 67.2; 75.1–2) which adds a sense of shared intimacy between the writer and his audience. This quality of personal, warm in-

formality, together with epigrammatic brevity and buoyancy, is a
mark of much of Seneca's philosophic writing and has earned for
him a perennial appeal. Quintilian, several decades after Seneca's
demise, observed that virtually Seneca alone among authors was
being read by the younger generation.[1] And this relaxed familarity
in him has continued to attract readers in almost every age, "and
constitute[s] Seneca," as Duff observes, "one of the most admirable essayists in the world."[2] He is virtually father of the essay, and
his influence upon the masters of this literary genre—Montaigne,
Bacon, Addison, Sainte-Beuve—is common knowledge.[3] Such easy
polish and finesse certainly rendered Seneca, as Ivar Lissner asserts, "one of the greatest educators of Western culture. . . ."[4]

Moreover, Seneca's evaluation of himself in his writings has a
significant psychological rightness about it. He was no elevated
and pompous lecturer, blind to error, glorifying an exalted and
unreal idealism. *Rectum iter,* he writes in the *Epistles, quod sero
cognovi et lassus errando, aliis monstro* ("the right road, which I
discovered late, and weary with wandering, I reveal to others,"
Ep. 8.3). There is a certain sad but keen introspective awareness
here, seldom discovered among moralists; for this Seneca wishes
to direct others to the proper path, yet fully recognizes that he
himself has hardly found it! Salted with irony and a certain realism, Seneca's assertions never ring with the falseness of an aloof
holdier-than-thou didacticism. He has so often, in others as in
himself, discovered weeds of human folly, not to mention the
veritable wilds and thickets of the human predicament.

Perhaps most remarkable in Seneca is the fact that, in an age
like his, he was conducting any quest at all. Since the founding of
the empire under Augustus in 31 B.C., almost a hundred years had
passed; aristocrats and intellectuals in Rome had witnessed the
deepening of absolutism with a corresponding deepening of
gloom. In the next century, Cornelius Fronto could look back and
observe the decline of oratory and language:

. . . Augustus was, I think, endowed with whatever elegance the century still retained and with whatever charm the Latin language still
possessed. . . . After Augustus, some remnants, already shriveled and
decayed, were left over for the disreputable Tiberius. But then the
emperors, right up to Vespasian, were all of such sort, that no less were
we ashamed of their oratory than we grieved at their character and
lamented their crimes.[5]

This sense of decline, of diminution, extends outward from the emperors to Roman culture itself. In literature,

What original work was produced in the days of Empire? It must be candidly admitted that after 120 we observe a diminuendo of production, as though increasing autocracy—what one contemporary called "being slaves of a well-meaning master"—was damping down creative spirit. There was little political or speculative writing, save some philosophical disquisitions on the rightness of monarchy, no great oratory, and no great poetry.[6]

In the first century, after the stellar appearance under Augustus of Horace, Vergil, Livy, Ovid, the remainder of that century at Rome appears bleak in letters indeed. Against this background of imperial intimidation and dismay, Seneca appears unique—a flower blooming in a field of Roman blades, all too easily in danger of being cut down: . . . *velut prati/ ultimi flos, praetereunte postquam/ tactus aratrost* ("like the flower on the verge of the field, after it has been struck by the passing plough").[7] His vast productivity in every literary kind—as philosopher, scientist, essayist, dramatist, satirist, poet, his capable wit and vigilant self-scrutiny, his sympathies, and his industry remind us of the ideal Renaissance man, a Leonardo da Vinci or a Sir Philip Sidney. No classic philosopher of his breadth and stature will appear again at Rome.

Because of this diversity in him, he has found favor in every age for one quality or another (though it must candidly be admitted that he has also found his denigrators; one cannot please all of the people all of the time). In the late empire, he was admired by the Christians. His personal touches, his humanitarian warmth, and particularly his assaults upon vice and his intense awareness of deity in the universe made him to the Church Fathers perhaps the most attractive of the pagans. He exerted, for instance, significant influence upon Tertullian, Lactantius, and St. Jerome; and, apparently in the fourth century, so close was Seneca's connection to the spirit of the Church felt to be that a spurious series of letters purporting to have been exchanged between Seneca and St. Paul was devised and long accepted as genuine.[8] Jerome's opinion, moreover (in the *De Viris Illustribus*), that Seneca was one of the early Christian writers, certainly enhanced the philosopher's popularity in the Church.[9]

In the Middle Ages, his precise, almost epigrammatic expressions led to his moral "sayings" being collected in commonplace books of "Seneks" and florilegia. His moral content and oratorical skill doubtless fostered the study of his rhetoric in the schools. For innumerable reasons, Seneca was certainly a towering influence in the Middle Ages, as the vast number of manuscripts and recensions of his works from the ninth through the fourteen centuries clearly attests. Seneca looms as an influential figure with a great number of medieval churchmen—Gregory the Great, John of Salisbury, Giraldus Cambrensis, Peter of Blois, Vincent of Beauvais, Bernard of Clairvaux, Alan of Lille, Abelard, and St. Bonaventure.[10]

As an interesting side note, during this medieval period, a prophetic choral passage in Seneca's *Medea* (375–79),

> A time will come in after years,
> when Ocean will loosen the shackles of things
> and the vast earth will be revealed
> and Tethys will disclose a new world
> and Thule will no longer be the Earth's boundary,

together with an inspiring one in the *Natural Questions* predicting future progress, was well heeded:

For how much space is there from the farthest shores of Spain to India? A distance of very few days, if a favorable wind attends the ship. (*N.Q.* Praef. 13)

The great scientist of the thirteenth century, Roger Bacon, cites this latter passage, in arguing for modern hopefulness and seeking to popularize a renaissance and pursuit of an idea of progress.[11] Subsequently, Christopher Columbus acknowledged that, inspired by these passages, he was induced to make the world-shaking voyage of 1492.[12] In fact, after the discovery of the New World, Seneca's supposed foreshadowing of such an event rendered him legendary. Thus, for instance, in the seventeenth century Thomas Pope Blount observes that the discovery of the Loadstone made the modern sea adventures possible: "we must then (for want of this Discovery) have committed our selves to the Sole conduct of the *Stars:* and as the *Ancients* did, must *We* always have been creeping near the Shoar: Then the fourth part of the

Earth had been yet unknown, and *Hercule's Pillars* had still been the World's *Ne Ultra: Seneca's* Prophecy had been an *unfulfill'd* Prediction, and one Moiety of our Globes an Empty Hemisphere."[13]

But, prophecy and discovery aside, Seneca's influence in many areas was felt in the Renaissance, as it had been in the Middle Ages. Seneca's habit of being independent, individualistic, forward-looking, and of debunking the rituals of superstitious religion rendered him inordinately popular with leading figures of the Renaissance—Petrarch, Erasmus, More, Vives, Reuchlin, Ascham, Quevedo, Lipsius, Calvin.[14] For many a sixteenth- and seventeenth-century leader, Seneca similarly represented the aristocratic ideal of the "courtier," whose vogue was again in the ascendant.[15] Needless to remark, Senecan style profoundly influenced Elizabethan and seventeenth-century authors,[16] just as his plays were a predominant source for the development of Elizabethan drama from the time of Jasper Heywood to the Jacobeans.[17] This dramatic influence extended itself into the neo-Classical period, when Corneille and Racine were writing, permeating and helping to shape the development of European theater.[18] And Stoic thought continued to be a moving force, as in the case of its influence upon Spinoza.[19]

In the eighteenth century, despite the influence of Shaftesbury,[20] Stocism, it is true, fell somewhat into disrepute; it was associated with skepticism and libertinism and frowned upon.[21] Later in the century, sentimentalism similarly looked with disapproval upon Stoic *apatheia* and the ideal of an almost emotionless self-control. Even so, Seneca still was a potent force upon the leading minds of the eighteenth century; as one critic has observed, this was the case with Samuel Johnson: "He cites Seneca and Epictetus more frequently than the philosophers of any other school, and he owned numerous editions of their works."[22] Furthermore, in the late eighteenth and early nineteenth centuries, Romanticism marked the revival of interest in Stoicism. Rousseau and his circle display the influence of Senecan and Stoic thought,[23] and Wordsworth was devoted to the concepts of the God that was in Nature, in fact citing Seneca in the epigraph to his "Ode to Duty" (1804).[24] Similarly, the romantic Transcendentalist movement, later in the century, owes much to the revivification of Stoic and Senecan ideals of self-reliance and deity that is simultaneously nature and reason, as readings in Emerson will illustrate.[25] Nevertheless, in the strictly "ethical" Victorian era, a number of critics—notably Macaulay—had chastised Seneca for a lack of staunch morality and an ostensibly vapid idealism.[26]

In the present century, however, Seneca is coming into his own. Dramatists early in the century—T. S. Eliot, Robinson Jeffers, Eugene O'Neill, Maxwell Anderson—had done much to revive interest in the stark and grim dramas of Euripides and Seneca, an interest that some of the dark scenes in recent drama of the so-called Theater of the Absurd, as in the work of Harold Pinter, has kept alive. But even more importantly, Seneca has become significant in philosophy. Advocates of Existentialism have become attracted to ideas that had challenged and preoccupied the Stoics: advocacy of an awareness of death, an engrossment in the problem of suicide, aloofness from a mad or absurd society, and a consequent revitalized sense of commitment to society and to man. Thus, all the major existentialist philosophers, from Kierkegaard to Jaspers and Heidegger, have been concerned with the boundaries of man's mortality and with questions of suicide and of death.[27] Camus' *Entre Plotin et Saint Augustin* (1936) and "Le Mythe de Sisyphe" (1942) establish his interest not only in Neoplatonism but also in Stoic endurance.[28] Likewise, Sartre's *L'Existentialisme est un humanisme* (1946), by emphasizing the dignity of man's making of himself and creating a morality of his own after suffering a crisis of conscience, reveals obvious links to Stoicism. Even Christian theologians, like Paul Tillich, attracted to Existentialism, have been motivated to reassess Stoicism, "the only real alternative to Christianity in the Western world," and to survey ideals of "courage" after man's having passed through anxiety, doubt, and despair.[29]

Perhaps the most recent and palpable instances of Seneca's presence among us in our day were the celebrations at Cordova and Madrid, in 1965, of the nineteenth-hundredth centennial of the philosopher's death. Scholars by the hundreds—from many disciplines—flocked from all over Europe and America into Spain for two separate celebrations, and subsequently, four volumes of papers, ovations, and commemorations have been published.[30]

Thus much for the wise and witty philosopher, the ardent moral teacher. This polymath's learning and humor shall not be forgotten; and he, perhaps, would have been best satisfied to have

been recognized as an instructor (and student) of ethical education. Perhaps Dante's designation of him, as *Seneca morale*,[31]
would have been gratifying, and certainly Chaucer's portrayal of
the philosopher as the ornament of the Neronian age would not
have been inappropriate or displeasing:

> In yowthe a maister hadde this emperour
> To teche hym letterure and curteisye,
> For of moralitee he was the flour,
> As in his tyme. . . .[32]

Notes and References

Chronology

1. For detailed studies of this question, see, for instance, E. Albertini, *La composition dans les ouvrages philosophiques de Sénèque* (Paris, 1923); A. Gercke, *Senecastudien* (Leipzig, 1896); and F. Giancotti, *Cronologia dei "Dialoghi" di Seneca* (Turin, 1957).

2. In listing these twelve *Dialogues,* I have followed the order given in the Ambrosian MS.

3. In listing the first nine tragedies, I have employed the order recorded in the Codex Etruscus. The last play, *Octavia,* appears in inferior MSS, and Senecan authorship is most doubtful.

4. Seventy-three epigrams in the *Anthologia Latina* have been attributed to Seneca. Only three of these have MS authority. Scholars have differed widely regarding the question of Senecan authorship. Duff, for example, believes "most, or indeed all, of the seventy-three may be his" (J. Wight Duff, *A Literary History of Rome in the Silver Age* [London, 1927], p. 246). Prato, on the other hand, makes no attempt to attribute any of them to Seneca; rather, he emphasizes the anonymous author's elegiac artistry (*Gli Epigrammi attribuiti a L. Anneo Seneca,* ed. & trans. Carlo Prato [Roma, 1964]).

5. For the testimony of ancient authors regarding Seneca's lost works and for fragments of these works, see *L. Annaei Senecae Opera Quae Supersunt,* ed. F. Haase (Leipzig, 1897), Vol. III, pp. 418–457.

6. Orations which Seneca delivered in the senate or wrote for the Emperor Nero.

Chapter One

1. Tacitus, *Annales* 15.67, words attributed to the tribune Subrius Flavus.

2. *Acts* 18:11–17.

3. He often alludes to general ill health, *Ep.* 61.1; 65.1; 67.2; but frequently mentions specific ills, fever (*Ep.* 104.1), asthma (*Ep.* 54.1–3,6), and catarrh (*Ep.* 78.1–4). It is generally thought that Seneca also suffered from consumption.

4. *Cf. Ep.* 58.5. For other references to the futility of such learning, see *Ep.* 78.37; 108.23–24; *De Brev. Vit.* 13.1–2.

5. Seneca the Elder, *Controversiae* 10.praef.2, 8, 9, 12.

6. *Iliad* 9.443.

7. Suetonius, *Caligula* 53.2.

8. *De Institutione Oratoria* 10.1.129.

9. Suetonius, *Caligula* 53.2.

10. Dio Cassius 59.19.7.

11. *De Ira* 1.20.8–9; 2.33.3 *sqq.;* 3.18.3–4; 3.19.

12. Dio Cassius 59.19.7.

13. Both Julia and Agrippina had been victims of the mad Caligula's wild debaucheries and had been banished by him after being dishonored. At the beginning of the new reign, their uncle Claudius recalled them from exile.

14. Dio Cassius 60.8.5–6; *Schol. Iuven.* 5.109.

15. Suetonius, *Claudius* 29. See also Seneca's *Apocolocyntosis* 10.4, and *cf. Octavia* 944–46.

16. Dio Cassius 60.8.5–6; Suetonius, *Claudius* 29; Tacitus, *Ann.* 14.63; *Apoc.* 10.4 and *Octavia* 944–46.

17. *Ad Polyb.* 13.2.

18. For a gruesome description of this island, consult *Ad Helv.* 6.5; 7.8. *Cf.* Seneca, *Epigr.* 1.

19. Eli Edward Burriss, *Seneca in Corsica* (New York, 1922), p. 25.

20. *Ad Helv.* 2.5. In this same Dialogue, 18.4–6, Seneca mentions a young child Marcus, *blandissimus puer,* whom some critics regard as another son of the philosopher, while others see in the boy Seneca's nephew, the future poet Lucan. At any rate, we can establish that Seneca was married prior to his banishment. Nothing, however, is known of his first wife. Since no mention is made of her in the *Ad Helv.*, one would surmise that she was already dead.

21. René Waltz, *Vie de Sénèque* (Paris, 1909), pp. 101–8; Italo Lana, *Lucio Anneo Seneca* (Turin, 1955), pp. 135–43; Richard Mott Gummere, *Seneca the Philosopher and his Modern Message* (Boston, 1922), p. 19.

22. *Ad Polyb.* 3.5; 7.1–4; 8.1–2; 12.3–5; 13.1–4; 14.1–2; 16.6.

23. *Ep.* 27.1; 57.3; 68.8–9; *De Vita Beata* 17.4; 18.1–2.

24. "Essai sur les Règnes de Claude et de Néron," IIe Partie, LXXXVIII & LXXXIX, in *Oeuvres de Denis Diderot* (Paris, 1821), XII, 52–54.

25. A. Momigliano, *L'opera dell'Imperatore Claudio* (Florence, 1932), pp. 135–42; W. H. Alexander, "Seneca's *Ad Polybium De Consolatione.* A Reappraisal," *Transactions of the Royal Society of Canada,* XXXVII (1943), 33–35.

26. In support of its authenticity, see Eugène Albertini, *La Composition dans les Ouvrages Philosophiques de Sénèque* (Paris, 1923), p. 20, n. 4.

27. Dio Cassius 60.14, 15, 18, 29.4–6; 60.31.2 (murder of Polybius); Suetonius, *Claudius* 29; Tacitus *Ann.* 11.1–3.

28. Tacitus, *Ann.* 11.26–38; Dio Cassius 60.31; Suetonius, *Claudius* 26.2; 29.3; 36.

29. Tacitus, *Ann.* 12.1–3; Suetonius, *Claudius* 26.3; Dio Cassius 60.31.5–8.

30. Tacitus, *Ann.* 12.3, 9; Dio Cassius 32.2.

31. Waltz, *Vie de Sénèque*, p. 125.

32. Tacitus, *Ann.* 12.8; Suetonius, *Nero* 7; Dio Cassius 60.32; *Schol. Iuven.* 5.109.

33. Tacitus, *Ann.* 15.63–64.

34. *Schol. Iuven.* 5.109.

35. Both Suetonius, *Nero* 6, and Dio, 61.3, report that, at Nero's birth, his father Domitius, foreseeing his son's future wickedness, exclaimed: "No good man could be born of Agrippina and myself."

36. Suetonius, *Nero* 52.

37. Tacitus, *Ann.* 13.2; cf. 14.55. See also *De Clem.* 1.13.4, where Seneca emphasizes the type of behavior suited to a ruler, and Suetonius, *Nero* 10.

38. Tacitus, *Ann.* 13.2.

39. Tacitus, *Ann.* 12.64–67; Suetonius, *Claudius* 44; Dio 60.34.

40. Tacitus, *Ann.* 12.68–69; Suetonius, *Claudius* 45; *Nero* 8; Dio 60.34.

41. Tacitus, *Ann.* 13.3. Since Tacitus is the only ancient source for Senecan authorship, some critics, like Concetto Marchesi, *Seneca* (Milan, 1934), pp. 44–45, and Carlo Pascal, *Seneca* (Catania, 1906), pp. 37–40, would deny that Seneca wrote this *laudatio funebris*. Their arguments are not based on fact and one might more readily believe Tacitus.

42. Dio 60.35.3.

43. Waltz, *Vie de Sénèque*, p. 143.

44. Tacitus, *Ann.* 13.2, 6, 11.

45. Dio 61.4.1.

46. Aurelius Victor, *De Caesar.* 5.2.

47. Tacitus, *Ann.* 13.4; Dio 61.3.

48. Tacitus, *Ann.* 13.5, 13–14.

49. Tacitus, *Ann.* 13.15–17.

50. Pliny, *Nat. Hist.* 14.4. For his popularity as a writer, see Quintilian, *Inst. Orat.* 10.1.126.

51. Tacitus, *Ann.* 13.18; Suetonius, *Nero* 34.1; Dio 61.8.4–6. And

indeed her power had been broken. Although Agrippina had at the outset of her son's reign been designated (unprecedentedly) *Augusta*, and even given predominance on imperial coinage upon which both mother and son appear, her falling-off was considerable. "After 55, her head and name never appeared on the Roman coinage again" (Michael Grant, *Nero: Emperor in Revolt* [New York, 1970], p. 48).

52. Tacitus, *Ann.* 13.19–22.

53. It was useless to remonstrate with Nero concerning his vices; see Dio 61.4–5. These vices included: his fondness for gladiatorial shows in which he coerced even senators and knights to participate (Dio 61.9; Suetonius, *Nero* 12); his addiction to performing music and reciting poetry repeatedly on the stage (Suetonius, *Nero* 20, 23; Dio 61.20); his custom of roaming the streets at night in disguise, molesting women, accosting young boys, brawling and even committing murder (Dio 61.9; Tacitus, *Ann.* 13.25; Suetonius, *Nero* 26).

54. Tacitus, *Ann.* 13.12, 45–46; Suetonius, *Otho* 3. Several modern critics believe that Poppaea is introduced by the ancient historians too early and that she was later, in 62 (at the time of Nero's ousting his wife Octavia), more conceivably present upon the scene.

55. Tacitus, *Ann.* 14.13.

56. Dio Cassius, almost always hostile to Seneca, claims (61.12.1) that Seneca urged Nero to commit this crime. Yet that seems most unlikely; Seneca's only motive could have been a fear of Agrippina's power and influence—but these had waned. She had been removed from court three years earlier, at which time her quest for predominance and authority had been abrogated. It is far more likely that the mother continued to haunt the son: the common reports of Nero's incest with Agrippina and of a kind of uncanny sway she wielded˙over her pampered and effeminate son suggest that the initiative to destroy this woman in 59 was Nero's. Consult B. H. Warmington, *Nero: Reality and Legend* (London, 1969), pp. 47–48.

57. Tacitus, *Ann.* 14.3–8; Dio 61.12–13; Suetonius, *Nero* 34.

58. Tacitus, *Ann.* 14.7, 10.

59. Tacitus, *Ann.* 14.10–11; Dio 61.14; Quintilian, *Inst. Orat.* 8.5.18.

60. *Ann.* 14.11.

61. *Ann.* 14.13.

62. Tacitus, *Ann.* 14.12–15, 20; on Nero's indulgence in theater and games, see Suetonius, *Nero* 12.

63. *Ann.* 14.12.

64. Tacitus, *Ann.* 14.51; Suetonius, *Nero* 35; Dio 62.13.

65. Suetonius, *Nero* 34.

66. Tacitus, *Ann.* 14.13.

67. His fear of authority figures is a point stressed in a fine analysis of Nero by Gilbert Charles-Picard, *Augustus and Nero: The Secret of Empire,* trans. Len Ortzen (New York, 1965), pp. 88–89.

68. J. P. Sullivan adduces much evidence of Petronian parodies of Seneca at this time and later: "Nero's court circle, like most coteries, was not without its literary—and political—undercurrents and conflicts, some of them, as Petronius learned to his cost, mortal" *(The Satyricon of Petronius: A Literary Study* [Bloomington, Indiana, 1968], p. 211).

69. Tacitus, *Ann.* 14.52–53.

70. *Ann.* 14.53–56.

71. Chester G. Starr, *Civilization and the Caesars: The Intellectual Revolution in the Roman Empire* (Ithaca, N.Y., 1954), p. 129.

72. Tacitus, *Ann.* 14.54.

73. Tacitus, *Ann.* 14.56.

74. *Ann.* 14.52.

75. *Ann.* 15.38; Suetonius, *Nero* 38.

76. *Ann.* 15.45; Dio 62.25.3. Dio likewise mentions Seneca's feigned illness and isolation, but adds (what there is little evidence for our accepting) that Seneca had in fact at this time surrendered all of his wealth to Nero, presumably to placate the emperor's vast craving to acquire funds for the fancy reconstruction of Rome.

77. *Ann.* 15.54.

78. *Ann.* 15.48, 65.

79. *Ann.* 15.49–50. The unreliable Dio, in a brief, confused account (62.24) names Seneca as one of the leading conspirators but makes no mention whatever of Piso! Suetonius *(Nero* 36) merely alludes with brevity to the *coniuratio pisoniana.*

80. *Ann.* 15.56.

81. *Ann.* 15.60.

82. *Ann.* 15.56.

83. Seneca regards Cato as worthy of the highest honor *(Ep.* 64.10) and refers repeatedly to his greatness. See *De Cons. Sap.* 7.1; 14.3; *De Ira* 2.32.2–3; 3.38.2; *De Vita Beata* 18.3; *De Tranq. An.* 7.5; 16.1; 17.9; *Ad Helv.* 9.5; 13.5; *Ad Marc.* 20.6; 22.3.

84. Tacitus, *Ann.* 15.60.

85. *Ann.* 15.61. For Seneca's criticism of flattery, see *Ep.* 59.11, 13; *De Ira* 2.21.7–8; *De Benef.* 6.30.3–6; *De Tranq. An.* 1.16; *N.Q.* 4.prol.3.

86. Tacitus, *Ann.* 15.62–64. His body was cremated without ceremony, in accordance with humble directions given much earlier when he had been at the height of wealth and power *(Ann.* 15.64).

87. Dio 62.25.

88. Tacitus, *Ann.* 15.63.

89. "Freud and the Future," *Freud, Goethe, Wagner* (New York, 1937), pp. 35–36.

90. Tacitus, *Ann.* 15.64.

91. Seneca himself frequently couples the noble deaths of Cato and Socrates naturally together; consult *Ep.* 13.4, 14; 67.7; 104.28–29; *De Tranq. An.* 7.5; 16.1; *De Prov.* 3.4. Cicero similarly associates Socrates with Cato, mentioning first the one, then the other (*Tusc. Disput.* 1.71–74). Even more importantly, Cato obviously understood himself to be following the "pattern" of Socrates; Plutarch reports that on the final evening of his life, Cato read through Plato's *Phaedo* (concerning Socrates' last day) twice (*Cato* 68, 70).

Later generations certainly perceived in Seneca but one further Socratic "pattern." In the only statue of Seneca now extant that distinctly bears his name (at the National Museum, Berlin), we find a double-bust, with Seneca's visage upon one side, Socrates' upon the other.

92. Tacitus, *Ann.* 15.62.

93. *Ann.* 15.62.

Chapter Two

1. Suetonius, *Nero* 35; Juvenal 10.16; Tacitus, *Annales* 13.42; 14.52, 53, 56; 15.64; Dio Cassius 61.10; 62.2, 25.

2. *Sat.* 10.16.

3. Tacitus, *Ann.* 14.52.

4. That Seneca was repelled by this popular type of philosopher is seen by *Ep.* 5.1–6. *Cf.* Horace, *Sat.* 1.3.133–36; 2.3.16, 35.

5. F. W. Farrar, *Seekers after God* (London, 1874), pp. 53–4.

6. *Ann.* 13.42.

7. R. Waltz, *Vie de Sénèque* (Paris, 1909), p. 389.

8. *Ann.* 13.42. In fact, Nero's own attitude toward Seneca was considerably altered. See W. H. Alexander, "The Tacitean 'non liquet' on Seneca," *University of California Publications in Classical Philology,* XIV, viii (1952), 322.

9. Dio 61.10.

10. Dio 61.10.

11. Dio 62.2. It is interesting to note that Tacitus (*Ann.* 14.30–39), who gives a detailed account of the rebellion in Britain, makes no mention of Seneca's name or of any usury.

12. *The History of Britain,* Bk. 2, from *The Prose Works of John Milton,* trans. C. R. Sumner (London, 1868), V, 208.

13. "Lord Bacon," *Critical and Historical Essays* (New York, 1875), p. 390.

14. *Seekers after God,* pp. 150, 148.

15. *A History of Roman Literature* (New York, 1887), p. 380.

16. *A Handbook of Latin Literature* (London, 1936), pp. 359–60.

17. "The Question of Seneca's Wealth," *Latomus* 14 (1955), 540, 544.

18. Tacitus, *Ann.* 13.43.

19. For endorsement of Tacitus' impartiality, reliability and worth as historian, see William Budham Donne, *Tacitus* (New York, 1883), p. 182; Henry Furneaux, Tacitus: *Annals I–IV* (Oxford, 1886), p. 7, and *The Annals of Tacitus* (Oxford, 1896), I, 31, 34; A. P. Ball, *Selected Essays of Seneca* (New York, 1916), p. xvi; C. Marchesi, *Seneca* (Messina, 1920), p. 142; V. Capocci, *Chi era Seneca* (Turin, 1955), pp. 26–30; Clarence W. Mendell, *Tacitus, the Man and His Works* (New Haven, 1957), pp. 219–22; Ronald Syme, *Tacitus* (Oxford, 1958), esp. I, 378ff., 398.

20. Tacitus, *Ann.* 13.42.

21. *Ann.* 13.43; 11.5.

22. Seneca's younger contemporary, Quintilian, in his *Inst. Orat.* 10.1.125–31, restricts himself solely to a discussion of the Senecan style.

23. *Ann.* 13.20; for other references in Tacitus to Fabius as historian, see 14.2; 15.61.6.

24. G. G. Ramsay, *The Annals of Tacitus* (London, 1909), II, 161 n. 1: "The fact that the wealth of Pallas is put at this same figure [300,000,000 sesterces] (12.53.5), as also by Dio (61.10.3), suggests that the number is a round one."

25. J. H. L. Wetmore, *Seneca's Conception of the Stoic Sage as Shown in His Prose Works* (Edmonton, Alberta, 1936), p. 48, explains: "Probably he did receive many legacies; he had the gift of making friends, and these would naturally remember him in their wills. Many, too, who were not friends, but who saw in him a person to be courted, would follow the custom of the day and name him as heir or joint heir. In all this, there was nothing inevitably sinister." And Farrar, *Seekers after God,* p. 54, points out that "it is not improbable that Seneca, like Cicero, and like all the wealthy men of their day, increased his property by lending money upon interest. No disgrace attached to such a course."

26. Suetonius, *Caligula* 53.2. Dio 59.19.7 also records this incident, in a passage remarkable for its praise of Seneca.

27. Tacitus, *Ann.* 14.53.

28. For a competent survey of such influence, see R. M. Gummere, *Seneca the Philosopher and His Modern Message* (Boston, 1922).

29. *Ep.* 82.10; 109.12; 117.9.

30. *De Benef.* 7.2.2; *Ep.* 76.19; 82.14; 94.8; *De Vita Beata* 4.3; 16.1.

31. *De Vita Beata* 22.4. For similar statements concerning wealth

and other indifferent things, consult *De Vita Beata* 22.1–2; 24.5; 25.1; *De Benef.* 5.13.2.

32. *Ep.* 4.7; 9.12; 13.11; 91.4–9; *Ad Marc.* 10.1.6; *Ad Polyb.* 2.7; 9.4; *De Benef.* 1.15.6; 3.22.4.

33. *Ep.* 18.13; 62.3; 92.31–2; 104.34; *De Vita Beata* 20.3; 21.1–2; *Ad Polyb.* 2.3.

34. Juvenal 5.108–10.

35. Martial 4.40; 12.36.

Chapter Three

1. For the prevalence of vice in men, see *Ep.* 7.1–7; 32.2; 75.15; 94.53–54; 95.23–24, 29, 33–34; 97.1–11; 99.13; *De Ira* 2.7.1–3; 2.8.1–3; 2.9.1–4; 2.10.1–5; 2.31.8; 3.26.3–5; *De Brev. Vit.* 2.3; 12.8; *Ad Polyb.* 13.1; *De Benef.* 1.10.1–4; 7.26.3–5; 7.27.1–3; *N.Q.* 1.17.10; 5.15.2; 7.31.2–3; 7.32.1–3; 4.prol.2.

2. *Ep.* 41.8; 76.9–11; 92.27; 113.17; 121.14; 124.14, 21, 23.

3. Eduard Zeller, *Die Philosophie der Griechen in ihrer Geschichtlichen Entwicklung* (Leipzig, 1923), Vol. III.i, p. 230.

4. *Ep.* 66.7; 71.4; 74.11–12; 76.19; *De Vita Beata* 15.5; *De Benef.* 4.2.2–3.

5. *Ep.* 57.3; 84.13; 85.26, 37–40; 111.4; 118.4; 119.12; *De Cons. Sap.* 5.4–7; 15.3–5; *De Tranq. An.* 11.1–2.

6. See esp. *Ep.* 44.7; 77.4, 13; 99.7; 102.24; 107.2; *De Vita Beata* 1.1–3; *De Brev. Vit.* 9.5; *Ad Polyb.* 11.2. Needless to say, the figure of the journey as indicator of quest and progress is common in literature; see, for example, Georg Roppen & Richard Sommer, *Strangers and Pilgrims: An Essay on the Metaphor of Journey* (Oslo, 1964).

7. *Rhetoric* 1354a.

8. *Ep.* 6.4; *cf. Ep.* 83, 90.1. For an especially thorough treatment of Seneca's conception (and the Greek tradition) of the philosopher as medicinal "healer-of-souls" *(Seelenarzt)*, consult Ilsetruat Hadot's *Seneca und die griechisch-römische Tradition der Seelenleitung* (Berlin, 1969).

9. See, e.g., *Ep.* 45.5–13; 48; 49.6–9; 82.9–24; 83.9–11, 17–18; 85.1–2; 87.40–41; 102.1–2, 4; 117.1, 19–20, 25–33.

10. The topic of the Hellenistic era and the beginnings of Stoicism is conveniently reviewed by Eduard Zeller, *Outlines of the History of Greek Philosophy*, 13th ed., trans. L. R. Palmer (New York, 1955), pp. 225–30.

11. See Richard M. Gummere's article stressing that Seneca was "more of an essayist than any other Roman," in his "The English Essay and some of its Ancient Prototypes," *Classical Weekly*, XIV (April 4, 1921), 154–60. For Senecan influence upon Montaigne, see *Essais*, esp. II.xxxii, "Defence de Sénèque et de Plutarque." In a canceled letter to

the Prince of Wales, Bacon similarly avows the debt of his essays to the *Epistulae Morales*; see *The Works of Francis Bacon,* ed. Basil Montagu (London, 1825), I, x.

12. See *Ep.* 6.5–6; 7.7; 83.13; 102.30; 104.21–22; 123.6; *De Ira* 2.21.9; 3.8.1–8; *De Tranq. An.* 1.12; *Ad Marc.* 2.1–2.

13. M. L. Clarke, *The Roman Mind: Studies in the History of Thought from Cicero to Marcus Aurelius* (New York, 1968), p. 124.

14. *Cf.* the similar idea in Donne's renowned meditation: "No man is an Island, entire of itself; every man is a piece of the Continent, a part of the main; if a Clod be washed away by the Sea, Europe is the less, as well as if a Promontory were, as well as if a Manor of thy friends or of thine own were; any man's death diminishes me, because I am involved in Mankind; and therefore never send to know for whom the bell tolls; it tolls for thee" ("Devotions Upon Emergent Occasions" XVII [1624]).

15. Here Seneca echoes the famous lines from Terence's *Heauton-timorumenos* 77: "Homo sum, humani nihil a me alienum puto." *Cf. De Ira* 1.5.2.

16. Anger resembles madness (*Ep.* 114.3); consult Seneca's treatise, *De Ira.* Cruelty, he argues, stems from anger (*De Ira* 2.5.1–5; 3.5.1–3; 3.19.5); this topic is treated most fully in the *De Clementia.*

17. Concerning the importance of kindliness to one's fellow men, see *Ep.* 48.7–8; 95.33, 51–52; 120.10; *De Ira* 1.5.2–3; 2.28.2; 2.34.5; 3.27.3; 3.43.5; *De Vita Beata* 20.3–4; 23.5; 24.1–3; *De Tranq. An.* 10.6; *De Clem.* 1.1.3–4; 2.6.2–3; *De Benef.* 1.2.4. The Stoics venerate no virtue more than kindness (*De Benef.* 1.15.2).

18. Early Fathers of the Church even accepted as genuine the forged correspondence between Seneca and St. Paul. See, for instance, H. N. Sevenster, *Paul and Seneca* (Leiden, 1961), and esp. P. Benoît, "Sénèque et Saint Paul," *Revue Biblique* LIII (1946), 7–35.

19. At one point, a knowing Seneca caustically asserts that old age is rarely achieved at court—unless one embrace injuries and obeisance (*De Ira* 2.33.2). For crucial Senecan comments about the necessity for contending with adversity, see *Ep.* 76.34–35; 78.17, 29; 91.3–4, 7–9, 15; 96.1–2; 98.5, 7; 99.32; 107.3–12; and all of the *De Providentia.*

20. See, for instance, G. Lowes Dickinson, "The Greek View of Women," in his *The Greek View of Life* [1896] (Ann Arbor, 1958), pp. 169–80. The topic is treated fully in Charles Seltman's *Women in Antiquity* (New York, 1949). See also "Women, Position Of" in *The Oxford Classical Dictionary,* 2d ed. (Oxford, 1970), pp. 1139–40.

21. See, for example, William L. Westermann, *The Slave Systems of Greek and Roman Antiquity* (Philadelphia, 1955), p. 116. His outspokenness on this subject has often been noted; thus, Samuel Dill remarks that "Seneca has never risen higher, or swept farther into the

future than in his treatment of slavery. He is far in advance of many a bishop or abbot or Christian baron of the middle age," *Roman Society from Nero to Marcus Aurelius* ([1905]; rpt. New York, 1957), p. 328.

22. *Ep.* 80.3; 95.33; *De Brev. Vit.* 12.2; 13.6–7; *De Clem.* 1.25.1.

23. *De Otio* 4.1; *Ep.* 28.5; 68.2; 102.21. For the traditions of the Cosmopolis, consult H. C. Baldry, *The Unity of Mankind in Greek Thought* (Cambridge, 1965).

24. *De Prov.* 1.1: "causam deorum agam." In Seneca *deus* and *dei* are used interchangeably. God is the supreme power that animates the universe, and the gods constitute different portions or manifestations of his activity.

25. *Ep.* 16.5; 58.27–28; 71.12, 14; 73.6; 107.9; *De Prov.* 1.2; 5.8; *De Vita Beata* 8.4; 20.5; *N.Q.* 5.18.5.

26. *Ep.* 90.1; 110.10; 113.16; *De Prov.* 5.8; *De Otio* 4.2; *Ad Helv.* 8.3; *Ad Marc.* 12.4; *De Clem.* 1.5.7; *De Benef.* 2.30.1; 4.6.1–6; 4.7.1; 7.31.2; *N.Q.* 5.18.5, 13; 7.30.3.

27. The assertion that God is synonymous with Fate has frequently led critics—wrongly, I believe—to accuse the Stoics of propagating determinism. Events in life may well be *fated* (they shall happen, eventually) without at all their having, of necessity, been determined (they *must* happen at a specific time). The importance Seneca attached to education, training, striving, and progression clearly indicates that he fully endorses what we would term "freedom of will." The distinction between "Fate" and "Necessity" in Stoicism, particularly with reference to Chrysippus, is well remarked by John M. Rist, *Stoic Philosophy* (Cambridge, 1969), Chap. 7.

28. *Ep.* 16.4–5; 65.12; *Ad Helv.* 8.3; *De Benef.* 4.7.1–2; 4.8.1–3; *N.Q.* 1.prol. 13–14; 2.45.1–3.

29. Eduard Zeller, *The Stoics, Epicureans and Sceptics*, trans. O. J. Reichel ([1879]; rpt. New York, 1962), p. 156. For discussion of the Stoic conception of periodic conflagration and destruction, followed by a reconstruction, of the universe, see E. Vernon Arnold, *Roman Stoicism* (Cambridge, 1911), pp. 190–93.

30. *Ep.* 65.2, 12–14, 23–24; 92.30; *De Vita Beata* 8.4; *N.Q.* 1.prol.13.

31. Wordsworth, "Lines Composed a few miles above Tintern Abbey . . ." (1798), lines 95–102.

32. Zeller, *Stoics, Epicureans and Sceptics*, 155–56; Arnold, *Roman Stoicism*, 180–82. The emphasis upon the primacy of the element fire was a Stoic borrowing from Heraclitus.

33. For a brief, intelligent treatment of these conceptions of God as simultaneously material stuff (*physis*) and spirit or *logos* in Zeno's thought, see Edwyn Bevan, *Stoics and Sceptics* (Oxford, 1913), pp. 40–42.

34. For a perceptive discussion of *logos*, consult Josiah B. Gould, "Reason in Seneca," *Journal of the History of Philosophy*, III (1965), 13–25.

35. Consult *Ep.* 123.16; *De Clem.* 2.5.1; *N.Q.* 6.29.3. We also possess fragments of Seneca's lost treatise, *De Superstitione.*

36. On the beneficent nature of God, cf. *Ep.* 95.49; *De Benef.* 7.31.4; and *De Ira* 2.27.1.

37. Samuel Johnson, *The History of Rasselas, Prince of Abissinia* (1759), Chap. 22. Living life "according to virtue" or "according to nature" is originally a Stoic phrase, but it is not an abstraction virtually incomprehensible. See Max Pohlenz, *Die Stoa: Geschichte einer geistigen Bewegung* (Göttingen, 1964), II, 67.

38. *Ep.* 47.15–16; 50.5–6; 73.16; 90.46; 94.29; 108.8; *De Benef* 5.22.1–4; 5.23.1–2; 5.25.5–6.

39. *Ep.* 42.1; cf. *De Tranq. An.* 7.4–5; *De Ira* 2.10.6; *De Cons. Sap.* 7.1.

40. *Ep.* 59.14; 73.12–15; *De Prov.* 1.5; *De Cons. Sap.* 8.2; *Ad Helv.* 5.2; *De Benef.* 7.3.2–3.

41. See References in note 40, above.

42. The state of wisdom appears very similar to paradise; see *Ep.* 75.18.

43. Readers interested in the topics of death and the afterlife among the Stoics should consult Ernst Benz, *Das Todesproblem in der Stoischen Philosophie* (Stuttgart, 1929).

44. Arnold, *Roman Stocism*, 267, citing this one passage, claims that Seneca here "definitely accepts" the doctrine of purgatory. But surely this must be called into question; rather, Seneca merely seems to be utilizing metaphoric language when he intimates that the newly risen spirit must adapt to its new environment slowly, pausing to "shake off" the cerements of mortality.

45. Plato, *Republic* 514A–521B; it is not surprising that in the *Ad Marciam De Consolatione* Seneca cites Plato's *Phaedo* 64A, where Socrates observes that the soul strives for, yearns for death and things beyond this life.

46. Cicero, *De Re Publica* 6.16–17. For the change during the Greco-Roman period in conception of the afterworld, removing it from underground, and situating it in "lunar" and "stellar" spheres above, see Franz Cumont, *After Life in Roman Paganism* (New Haven, 1922), Chapters 2 and 3.

47. Lucretius, *De Rerum Natura* 3.838–53, 862–69. The translation is John Dryden's, from *Sylvae* (1685).

48. On the doctrine of periodic conflagration and renewal of creation, consult Seneca, *N.Q.* 3.13.1, 27–28. Cf. Cicero, *De Nat. Deorum* 2.118; *De Re Publica* 6.21; *Tusc. Disp.* 1.31. Actually, various Stoics

were in disagreement among themselves concerning doctrines of conflagration and immortality of the soul; see Arnold, *Roman Stoicism*, 267–68, and Zeller, *Stoics, Epicureans and Sceptics*, 217–18.

49. Seneca here is asking Marcia to imagine that her dead father, Aulus Cremutius Cordus, is speaking to her from a grand height and almost divine vantage point.

50. Plato, *Apology* 40C–41C.

51. *Paul and Seneca*, p. 225, alluding to Seneca's *De Tranq. Am.* 14.7–8. Sevenster's discussions of Seneca's relation to the topics of death (pp. 219–23), the afterlife (pp. 224–29), and suicide (pp. 52–57) are all intelligently handled.

52. "Life of Milton," *Lives of the English Poets* (London, 1925), I, 63. Admittedly, Seneca's interests (like Johnson's) did not exclude the study of biology and astronomy, but these studies were pursued only to the extent that they informed one about God and his laws. Strabo, Posidonius, and other Stoics had done much to elevate the dignity and significance of scientific studies.

53. Epictetus, frag. 175, Schweighaüser edition.

54. See *Ep.* 54.1–3, 6; 61.1; 65.1; 67.1–2; 78.1–4; 104.1. On the effect of such sad and painful personal experience upon Seneca, consult E. Busch, "*Fortunae resistere* in der Moral des Philosophen Seneca," *Antike und Abendland*, X (1961), 131–54.

55. The standard study on this subject in antiquity is Rudolf Hirzel, "Der Selbstmord," *Archiv. für Religionswissenschaft*, XI (1908), 75–104, 243–84, 417–76. Modern existentialist thought has once again rendered the near approaches of death philosophically significant. "Man does not know his humanity until he proves it by courage and by contempt for death," affirms Karl Jaspers, *The Future of Mankind*, trans. E. B. Ashton (Chicago, 1958), p. 42.

56. *Ep.* 58.36, 98.18; 24.23, 70.8; 24.22, 24, 26, *De Tranq. An.* 2.15.

57. *Ep.* 78.2; 98.15–16; 104.3–4.

58. It should be remembered that such Stoic leaders as Zeno, Cleanthes, Antipater of Tarsus, Cato the Younger themselves committed suicide.

59. *Ep.* 30.2, 58.33–35; *De Benef.* 7.20.3; *Ep.* 58.36, 98.16; 17.9; *De Ira* 3.15.3–4.

60. Albert Salomon, *In Praise of Enlightenment* (New York, 1963), p. 16.

61. Cato is again and again extolled: see *Ep.* 13.4; 24.6–8; 67.7, 13; 70.19, 22; 71.16–17; 82.12–13; 95.72; 104.29, 32; *Ad Marc.* 22.3; *De Tranq. An.* 16.1, 4; *De Prov.* 2.9–12; 3.4.

62. John M. Rist, *Stoic Philosophy*, pp. 246–51, writes of Seneca's "exoticism," his "obsession" with suicide as being atypical of Stoicism,

since Seneca offers "virtually a paean to suicide." We may suspect that this viewpoint is much exaggerated.

63. *Ep.* 4.4; 32.4–5; 49.10; 58.34; 61.4; 70.5–6; 74.26–27; 77.4, 6, 20; 78.27–28; 85.22–23; 92.25; 93.2–8, 11–12; 101.15; *Ad Marc.* 24.1; *De Brev. Vit.* 7.9–10; *De Benef.* 5.17.6.

64. Plutarch, "Regum et imperatorum apophthegmata," *Moralia* 194A.

65. Herodotus, *Histories* 1.32. The sentiment is echoed in the famous last chorus of the *Oedipus Tyrannus,* 1529–30.

66. W. D. Nietmann, "Seneca on Death: The Courage To Be or Not To Be," *International Philosophical Quarterly,* VI (1966), 89.

67. Samuel Dill, *Roman Society from Nero to Marcus Aurelius* ([1905]; rpt. New York, 1957), p. 343; consult the section on "Eclecticism" in Eduard Zeller's *Outlines of the History of Greek Philosophy,* trans. L. R. Palmer ([13th ed. rev., 1931]; rpt. New York, 1955), pp. 264–84.

68. Arnold, *Roman Stoicism,* pp. 106–107.

69. E.g., C. S. Rayment, "Echoes of the Declamations in the Dialogues of the Younger Seneca," *Classical Bulletin,* XLV (1969), 51–52, 63.

70. E.g., Pierre Grimal, "Sénèque et la pensée grecque," *Bulletin de l'Association G. Budé,* sér. 4 (1966), 317–30.

71. Pierre Thévenaz, "L'intériorité chez Sénèque," in *Mélanges offerts à M. Max Niedermann* . . . (Neuchatel, 1944), pp. 189–96. The article's one weakness occurs at the close; Thévenaz's Christianity allows him to discount Senecan thought.

72. A. Cattin, "Sénèque et l'astronomie," *Latomus,* XLIV (*Hommages à Léon Hermann,* 1960), 237–43; G. Faggin, "Il Misticismo Astrale di Seneca," *Atene e Roma,* n.s. 12 (1967), 23–37.

73. C. J. Herington, "Senecan Tragedy," *Arion,* V (1966), 422–71; esp. pp. 433 ff.

Chapter Four

1. For the most useful of such studies, see John W. Cunliffe's lucid volume, *The Influence of Seneca on Elizabethan Tragedy* (London, 1893), and also F. L. Lucas, *Seneca and Elizabethan Tragedy* (Cambridge, 1922).

2. For a detailed citation of such hostile criticism, consult Howard V. Canter, "Rhetorical Elements in the Tragedies of Seneca," *University of Illinois Studies in Language and Literature,* Vol. X (Urbana, Illinois, 1925), pp. 15–18. One of the most severe critics has been Désiré Nisard, *Études de moeurs et de critique sur les Poëtes latins de la Décadence* . . ., 2d ed. (Paris, 1849), esp. pp. 57–144.

3. "Seneca in Elizabethan Translation," *Selected Essays* (New York,

1950), pp. 58, 60. However, critics have too often opposed the examination of individual plays by and for themselves. There are two
general "schools" of criticism of Senecan tragedy; one that finds his
work wholly derivative from Greek drama, and another that urges his
Roman (and particularly his Stoic) qualities. Typical of the first, Greek-
ish, school would be Pierre Grimal's "L'originalité de Sénèque dans la
tragédie de *Phèdre*," *Revue des Études Latines*, XLI (1963), 297–314,
who ironically discovers Seneca's "originality" to be the yoking of
Euripidean sources together, and William M. Calder III, "Originality
in Seneca's *Troades*," *Classical Philology*, LXV (1970), 75–82, who discovers no originality whatever. The second school would rescue Seneca
from Greece, and Romanize him as much as possible; see, for instance,
R. B. Steele, "Some Roman Elements in the Tragedies of Seneca,"
American Journal of Philology, XLIII (1922), 1–31, and Moses Hadas,
"The Roman Stamp of Seneca's Tragedies," *American Journal of
Philology*, LX (1939), 220–31. It is quite popular for the critic to go
still further, and to discover deeper and deeper layers of a pervasive
Roman Stoicism in the plays; see especially Norman T. Pratt, Jr., "The
Stoic Base of Senecan Drama," *Transactions of the American Philo-
logical Association*, LXXIX (1948), 1–11, who discerns philosophic
"teachings" in the tragedies, and Berthe Marti, "Seneca's Tragedies.
A New Interpretation," *Transactions of the American Philological
Association*, LXXVI (1945), 216–45, who finds the entire Senecan
dramatic corpus arranged in a progressive order of instructive Stoical
lessons. The point, of course, is not that Seneca is free of Greek or
Roman influences, but that he has made of them something of his own.

    4. Perhaps too much emphasis is placed upon blood and horror.
See, for instance, Gareth Lloyd-Jones, "Shakespeare, Seneca, and the
Kingdom of Violence," in *Roman Drama*, ed. T. A. Dorey & D. R.
Dudley (New York, 1965), pp. 123–59, who designates much of this
violence "sensationalism." But we must remember that *all* tragedies
are in some measure bloody and violent; we will need to qualify this
broad conception of rage and turbulence in Senecan drama.

    5. Most noteworthy, concerning such bloody catastrophes, is the
tendency in Seneca to dismember his victims. One thinks of Astyanax'
broken body after his fall in the *Troades*, of Hippolytus torn in bits
in the *Phaedra*, and the dissected children served up at a feast in the
Thyestes.

    6. A good case may also be made for the very different standards
appreciated by Roman audiences, particularly a taste for mime, opera,
melodrama, and pageant. See E. F. Watling, Introduction to Seneca,
Four Tragedies and Octavia (Baltimore, 1966), pp. 17–21, and Moses
Hadas, "The Roman Stamp of Seneca's Tragedies," *American Journal
of Philology*, LX (1939), 220–31.

7. Too few critics have spoken enough of Seneca's art. Norman T. Pratt, Jr., *Dramatic Suspense in Seneca and in His Greek Precursors* (Princeton, 1939), did undertake to examine some of the dramatic artistry in the prologues to the plays, yet elsewhere he adjudges Senecan drama "second-rate melodrama," its Stoic elements "too simple and shallow" to account for human behavior or even to allow for tragedy—without giving the plays a very careful look ("Tragedy and Moralism: Euripedes and Seneca," in *Comparative Literature: Method and Perspective*, ed. N. P. Stallknecht & H. Frenz [Carbondale, Illinois, 1961], pp. 199, 202).

8. Although, ironically enough, we must perceive that even here, at the time of her children's demise, Medea's lunatic sense of revenge is not fully satiated; she considers the number of children slaughtered "too small" for her revenge (lines 1010–11). Perhaps revenge can *never* be fully achieved. At any rate, in the next shocking image, she offers to go even further—to plunge the sword into herself and to scourge her own womb! (lines 1012–13).

9. Denis Henry and B. Walker, "Loss of Identity: *Medea Superest?* A Study of Seneca's *Medea*," *Classical Philology*, LXII (1967), 169–81, correctly (I believe) perceive that the *Medea* studies not horrible action but intensity of character, and they rightly assess Medea's projected mental paths of escape as "blind alleys." However, they overemphasize the play's "moral vacuum" and do not discuss the ironies attending Medea's "vengeance."

10. Ernst Robert Curtius, *European Literature and the Latin Middle Ages*, trans. W. R. Trask ([1948]; rpt. New York, 1963), pp. 94–98.

11. Bertha S. Phillpotts, "Wyrd and Providence in Anglo-Saxon Thought," *Essays & Studies by Members of The English Association*, ed. Caroline Spurgeon (Oxford, 1928), p. 12.

12. *Poetics* 6.1449b and 9.1452a.

13. Such a "balancing" of opposing forces in tragedy's conflict has been frequently noted by critics; Henry Alonzo Myers, *Tragedy: A View of Life* (Ithaca, New York, 1956), p. 72, speaks of the "equivalence" in tragedy of victory and defeat. Donald A. Stauffer, *The Golden Nightingale: Essays on Some Principles of Poetry in the Lyrics of William Butler Yeats* (New York, 1949), p. 98, proposes the tragic poet's paradoxically "double" awareness of limitations *and* infinite capabilities in his creations. Such an equilibrium is perhaps that very quality that defines "tragic irony," what I. A. Richards designates the "bringing in of the opposite" (*Principles of Literary Criticism* [New York, n.d.], pp. 245–53).

14. Michael Ayrton, *The Maze Maker* (New York, 1967), pp. 242–44.

15. It may well be urged, nonetheless, that some Senecan characters do indeed appear "fated." Gerhard Müller has rightly discriminated in

Seneca's theater "tragedies of passion" (*Medea, Phaedra*) as well as "tragedies of fate" (*Thyestes, Oedipus*). Consult Müller's "Senecas *Oedipus* als Drama," *Hermes*, LXXXI (1953), esp. 460. Still, it can be argued that *all* Senecan protagonists, though in some sort "driven," nevertheless display serious defects of character and perversion of choice.

16. Homer, *Odyssey* 8.577–80.

Chapter Five

1. Horace, *Epist.* 1.13–19. It is certainly true that the Roman satirists—and philosophers like Seneca—inherited much of this witty tone from the Greek Cynics and their diatribes. For the influence of the Cynic Bion upon the satirists, see George Converse Fiske, *Lucilius and Horace* ([1920]; rpt. Hildesheim, 1966), esp. pp. 178–201. Donald R. Dudley, in *A History of Cynicism* ([1937]; rpt. Hildesheim, 1967), pp. 66 ff., translates some fragments of Bion that give us a sense of his jaunty and conversational tone. For an overview of this whole topic, consult André Oltramare, *Les Origines de la Diatribe Romaine* (Geneva, 1926). Chap. 11, in fact, deals with Seneca.

2. See also *Ep.* 12.11. For the more conservative Old Testament view, consult Jeremiah 6:16.

3. A Senecan gambit was his repeated recital and endorsement of the sayings of Epicurus; Epicurus is quoted or cited, sometimes more than once, in twenty-seven of the first thirty-three *Epistulae Morales;* consult Anna Lydia Motto & John R. Clark, "*Paradoxum Senecae:* The Epicurean Stoic," *Classical World*, LXII (1968), 37–42.

4. *Essais*, 2.32.

5. Anthony Ashley Cooper, Third Earl of Shaftesbury, *Characteristics of Men, Manners, Opinions, Times* (1711), 6.1.3n.

6. Robert Frost, "Two Tramps in Mud Time," lines 66–67.

7. E.g., consult *De Otio* 3.2–3, where Epicurean and Stoic views of the active life are contrasted. Seneca holds that Epicurean *voluptas*, a self-seeking privateness, an effete repose, "is the good of cattle" (*Ep.* 92.6).

8. Seneca exhorts withdrawal from the crowd into private life, *Ep.* 19.8; 20.1, 6–8; 21.1–6; 22.1–12; 68.1; one should particularly seek solitude to escape the crowd, 25.7; and one should devote such solitude to study, 94.72.

9. *Ep.* 103.5: "But you must never boast of philosophy; when used with insolence and arrogance, it has been dangerous to many." *Ep.* 25.5: "solitude induces us to evils of every kind." One should not seek Epicurean isolation, *Ep.* 68.10–11, nor is solitude safe for fools, *Ep.* 10.2. At best, one must almost be the Stoic *sapiens* to render solitude fruitful, *Ep.* 25.7.

10. *Ann.* 14.52.

11. *Ann.* 13.3.

12. *Ann.* 12.2.

13. *Ann.* 15.62.

14. See *Ep.* 3.5–6; 14.14–15; 68.1; *De Otio* 2.1–2; 3.1; *De Tranq. An.* 17.3.

15. Oct. 27, 1818, to Richard Woodhouse, *The Selected Letters of John Keats,* ed. Lionel Trilling (New York, 1956), p. 166.

16. On *decorum personae,* see Aristotle, *Poetics* 15.1454a15–19; Horace, *Ars Poetica* 112–18, 153–78, 227–30. For the concept's influence in the neo-Classical period, consult René Bray, *La Formation de la doctrine classique en France* (Paris, 1961), pp. 215–30.

17. Typifying the double standard of artistic withdrawal and public activity in his later life is his dwelling in the isolated Norman tower of Thoor Ballylee, on the one hand, and his involvement as senator in the newly formed Irish Free State on the other. An admirable treatment of such internal debates in his poetry may be found in Richard Ellman's "Robartes and Aherne: Two Sides of a Penny," *Kenyon Review,* X (1948), 177–86.

18. C. G. Jung, *Modern Man in Search of a Soul,* trans. W. S. Dell & C. F. Baynes (New York, 1933), pp. 95–97. *Cf.* Freud's later conception of the primal antagonism between Eros (Life Wish) and Thanatos (Death Wish) in *Beyond the Pleasure Principle* (1920). The reconciliation, by art, of Eros and Thanatos is developed by Herbert Marcuse, *Eros and Civilization* (New York, 1961), pp. 149, 157–79.

19. There is the further irony that it is "Serenus" who suffers from vacillation and flux.

20. *De Providentia* is full of paradoxical praise for adversity; see also *Ep.* 13.1–3; 94.74; 110.3; *Ad Marc.* 5.2; *Ad Helv.* 2.3.

21. *Ep.* 99.17; 102.13; all of 97 and 103; *De Clem.* 1.1; *De Tranq. An.* 15.2–5. The traditional Stoic paradox, of course, insisted that "All but the Wise are mad."

22. For Seneca's views on suicide, consult the discussion, above, in Chapter 3, pp. 74–77.

23. The existentialist's belief in the necessity of a confrontation with death is treated in William Barrett's *Irrational Man* (New York, 1958), pp. 200–203. One might recall Carlyle's mystical crisis, which moved through a despairing "Everlasting No," into a "Center of Indifference," and thence to the affirmative "Everlasting Yea" in *Sartor Resartus* (1833–34). Philosophically, the two phases, negative and positive, are treated consecutively in Martin Heidegger's *Sein und Zeit* (1929) and *Platons Lehre von der Wahrheit* (1942). The best literary dramatizations of these phases may be found in Albert Camus' *L'Etranger* (1942), whose meaninglessness and despair should be con-

trasted with his short stories of affirmation, "L'Hôte" and "La Pierre qui pousse" in *L'Exil et le royaume* (1957).

24. Plato makes this point in the *Republic* 9.592.

25. *Brutus* 46.170–71.

26. *Serm.* 2.7.

27. The *tympanum* or tambourine was associated with the castrated priests of the orgiastic Eastern cult of the goddess Cybele. Ironically, Seneca's protest that the Epicureans retain their masculinity is gracefully ludicrous and certainly ambivalent.

28. Plato, *Symposium* 215A–B. Cf. Seneca's descriptions of Claranus, *Ep.* 66.1–4.

29. General interest in "play" in culture, and particularly in literature, is distinctly coming to the fore. See Johan Huizinga, *Homo Ludens: A Study of the Play-Element in Culture* (Boston, 1955), esp. pp. 120, 122–27; and Josef Pieper, *Leisure, the Basis of Culture* (New York, 1964), pp. 17, 29, 30, 46. Concerning the playfulness in particular eras and authors, see, for instance, Paul Friedländer, *Plato: An Introduction* (New York, 1958), pp. 118, 123, 137–53; Herman Sinaiko, *Love, Knowledge, and Discourse in Plato* (Chicago, 1965), pp. 114–18; K. J. McKay, *The Poet at Play: Kallimachos, The Bath of Pallas* (Leiden, 1962); Zoja Pavlovskis, "Aristotle, Horace, and the Ironic Man," *Classical Philology*, LXIII (1968), 22–38; Georg Luck, "*Vir Facetus*: A Renaissance ideal," *Studies in Philology*, LV (1958), 107–21; Frank J. Warnke, "Sacred Play: Baroque Poetic Style," *Journal of Aesthetics and Art Criticism*, XXII (1964), 455–64.

30. The Stoics from the beginning engaged in logical paradoxes, the most famous being the Liar: the person who asserts that he is lying is both lying *and* telling the truth. Such paradoxes were often framed as syllogisms, thus:

> The Horns
> What you have not lost, you still retain.
> You have not lost your horns.
> Therefore, you still retain horns.

Consult Benson Mates, *Stoic Logic* (Berkeley & Los Angeles, 1961), pp. 84–85. But the Stoics utilized paradoxes far more broadly, wielding them as weapons in disputation to shock auditors to attention and awareness. Thus the Stoics commonly insisted that "All but the Wise Man are mad," that "Only the Wise Man is king," that "Riches are an 'indifferent' thing," that "Pain is not an evil," that "The Wise Man cannot receive an injury," and that "Adversity is beneficial to man." Consult Cicero's collection of exercises arguing several such theses, the *Paradoxa Stoicorum*.

31. Seneca condemns philosophers who extend philosophy to in-

clude grammar, philology, history, poetics—*Ep.* 88.2–3; cf. 108.35.
He generally scorns sophistic oratory and sophistic reasoning—*Ep.* 48;
88.42–45; 111; and he parodies such practice in *Ep.* 106. Philosophers,
he feels, should never yield to ostentation and concern for public relations, *Ep.* 68.3.

Ultimately, Seneca recommends an intellectual honesty reminiscent
of Hamlet's advice to the Players: philosophers should "suit the action
to the word, the word to the action"; eloquence by itself is an empty
goal, *Ep.* 75.3–5. Rather than a vain or vociferous oratory, Seneca in
the *Epistulae Morales* prefers quiet "conversation": *Ep.* 38.1; cf. 67.2.

32. He terms most paradoxes "*mirabile*" and "*incredible*," *De Benef.*
2.31.1; cf. his summary of traditional practice in Stoic paradoxes, *De
Benef.* 2.35.2–3. An *adversarius* adequately states the case against
Stoic paradoxes in *De Cons. Sap.* 3.1–2; cf. *Ep.* 81.11–12. Seneca's
most comic treatment of paradox envisions a silly "thinker" who,
even as the enemy overrun his city with fire and sword, sits idle, reciting the paradoxical syllogism of the Horns, *Ep.* 49.7–8.

33. *Vid.* his attack upon pseudo-Stoic sophistries, *Ep.* 123.15–16;
or the *reductio ad absurdum* of the syllogism in *Ep.* 48.4–7. For criticism of Zeno's syllogisms, see *Ep.* 82.9–10, 19–20; 83.9–11.

34. Seneca protests that, at best, he himself is a *proficiens* (i.e., one
on the path of moral progress): consult *Ep.* 6.1–4; 8.1–3; 57.3; 63.14;
68.8–9; 87.4–5; *De Vita Beata* 17.3–20.6; 24.4. On the term *proficiens*
itself, *vid. Ep.* 71.30.

35. *Ep.* 42.1; cf. *De Cons. Sap.* 7.1; *De Ira* 2.10.6; *De Tranq. An.*
7.4.

36. Exemplary of the "clinical" approach is E. Phillips Barker on
"Seneca" in *The Oxford Classical Dictionary* (Oxford, 1949), 827–28.
Barker finds Seneca "neurotic," displaying the "common stigmata of
paranoic abnormality." His prose as a consequence is certainly not
coherent, consistent, or "architectonic," but rather "spasmodic." [A
much improved article on "Seneca," by Reynolds and Ker, replaces
Barker's in the *Oxford Classical Dictionary*, 2d ed., 1970, pp. 976–77.]
Writers like H. J. Rose revile Seneca's morals and then debunk his
prose. Seneca is found essentially a rhetorician, his prose "wearisome,"
possessing "neither depth of thought, real originality, nor the power
to become perfectly plain and simple . . ." (*A Handbook of Latin Literature* [London, 1936], p. 370).

37. Indeed, Seneca in the second letter (*Ep.* 2.4) had "promised"
such a flurry of quotations. Even though he advises against scattered
reading in this second epistle, Seneca nevertheless commences to offer
in every letter a "thought for the day." Such a daily portion is variously
termed: "*dicta*" (7.10), "*mercedula*" (6.7), "*peculium*" (12.10), "*prae-
ceptum*" (15.9).

38. Such criticism of maxims is foreshadowed by warnings against vacillation and agitation generally, *Ep.* 32.2.

39. God himself is *"artifex";* what better than that artists in their work, and the *sapiens* in his life, imitate the deity? "By Hercules, it is the mark of a great artist to have enclosed all in a little space" (*Ep.* 53.11).

40. "Simplex et unum" are Horace's terms of approbation for works of art, *Ars Poetica* 23.

41. One thinks of the noisy, crowded cities in Theocritus' 15th *Idyll*, in Juvenal 3, in Swift's "Description of a Morning." On the subject is Arthur Schopenhauer's excellent little essay "Über Lärm und Geräusch," in his *Parerga und Paralipomena* (1851).

42. *Aeneid* 2.726–29.

43. This would have seemed right to Romans; indeed, the figure of a heroic Aeneas dedicated to his family, carrying his father, and leading his son, was doubtless popular in the empire—illustrative of *pietas*. See the wall painting of just this group recovered at Pompeii and now at the Museo della Civiltà Romana.

44. Seneca lightly intimates comparison of himself with Odysseus throughout the epistle; vapors and bathhouse are equated with waves and ocean voyage. The note of mock-epic analogy is distinct.

45. Anthony Ashley Cooper, Earl of Shaftesbury, *"Sensus Communis:* An Essay on the Freedom of Wit and Humour," *Characteristics of Men, Manners, Opinions, Times,* ed. J. M. Robertson ([1711]; rpt. Indianapolis, 1964), I, 44, 49, 52, *passim.* Consult A. O. Aldridge, "Shaftesbury and the Test of Truth," *Publications of the Modern Language Association,* LX (1945), 129–56.

46. *Histories* 2.173. For a further account of Amasis' philosophy of "balance," consult his letter to Polycrates, 3.40. The idea of such a mixture of work and play is commonplace, as in Horace, *Odes* 4.12.27–28.

47. "The Sense of the Sleight-of-Hand Man," lines 1–2.

48. Seneca is alluding to the tale of Phaëthon's attempting to drive his father's, the sun-god's, chariot—recounted at the outset of Book II of Ovid's *Metamorphoses*.

Chapter Six

1. Literally, "We give ourselves to the breeze to be carried"; Seneca's succinctness can hardly be rendered, let alone be imitated, in English.

2. Quintilian, but a generation after Seneca, acknowledges that Seneca's writings were the rage among the young and, although he disapproves of Senecan style, observes Seneca's "multae claraeque sententiae" and "minutissimae sententiae" (*Inst. Orat.* 10.1.129–30). Similarly, Abraham Cowley in the seventeenth century speaks of "the dry chips of short lung'd Seneca" ("Ode. of Wit" [1656], line 52). And

Erasmus observes that "Truly, from Seneca's reflections you can find something to imitate more easily than from others where maxims are neither frequent nor striking" ("Ciceronianus" [1528], quoted in Izora Scott, *Controversies over the Imitation of Cicero* [New York, 1910], Pt. II, p. 37). For a recent examination of Senecan style, see H. Mac L. Currie, "The Younger Seneca's Style: Some Observations," *Bulletin of the Institute of Classical Studies* (University of London), XIII (1966), 76–87.

3. Walter C. Summers discusses "The Pointed Style in Greek and Roman Literature" in his edition of *Select Letters of Seneca* (London, 1910) pp. xv–xli. He attributes "pointed" style, among others, to Timaeus, Bion, Menippus, Cato the Elder, Ovid, Sallust. See also C. N. Smiley, "Seneca and the Stoic Theory of Literary Style," *Classical Studies in Honor of Charles Foster Smith* (Wisconsin Studies in Language & Literature, no. 3; Madison, 1919), pp. 50–61.

4. *Ep.* 5.1 opens with reference to *omnibus omissis*, "omitting all things," which characteristically offers an example of alliteration as well as antithesis that approaches oxymoron.

5. Seneca upon several occasions observes that he wishes his prose to be informal, easy, conversational; see *Ep.* 67.2; 75.1–2.

6. On the considerable influence of Senecan style in the Renaissance, see Morris W. Croll, *Style, Rhetoric, and Rhythm* (Princeton, 1966), and George Williamson, *The Senecan Amble* (Chicago, 1951). Recently, the theories of Williamson and Croll, that anti-Ciceronianism was widespread and reflected in many styles, and that Stoicism and Senecan style were especially popular in England from 1580 to 1630, are being re-examined and modified; see Brian Vickers, *Francis Bacon and Renaissance Prose* (Cambridge, 1968), esp. pp. 106–15, and Earl Miner, "Patterns of Stoicism in Thought and Prose Styles, 1530–1700," *Publications of The Modern Language Association*, LXXXV (1970), 1023–34.

7. The two most important studies of *De Providentia* are both concerned with *oratio*. Pierre Grimal's "La Composition dans les 'dialogues' de Sénèque. II.—Le *De Providentia*," *Revue des Études anciennes*, LII (1950), 238–57, offers a rhetorical analysis of the work, according to divisions of traditional oratory (*exordium, narratio, confirmatio*, etc.). Karlhans Abel's study, in his *Bauformen in Senecas Dialogen* (Heidelberg, 1967), pp. 97–123, presents a similar rhetorical analysis, Abel arguing that the dialogue includes a proemium and epilogue. Both authors stress rhetorical organization and delivery, although Abel's study is also concerned with questions of logic, psychology, and philosophy as well. The present analysis, unlike these, is concerned not with rhetorical but with literary structure and form.

8. *Stoicorum Veterum Fragmenta*, ed. J. von Arnim, 4 vols. ([1905]; rpt. Stuttgart, 1964), II, 284, frag. 975, attributed to Zeno and

Chrypsippus. Cf. frag. 527, attributed to Cleanthes, which Seneca cites in *Ep.* 107.11. Consult M. Marcovich, "On the Origin of Seneca's *Ducunt volentem fata, nolentem trahunt*," *Classical Philology,* LIV (1959), 119–21.

9. Seneca was himself attracted to this Heraclitean metaphor of time and the river; see *Ep.* 58.23.

10. Traditional terminology for the "parts" of the oration are reviewed in Cicero's *De oratore* 2.78.315–2.81.333.

11. For recent explorations of the dramatic qualities in Senecan prose, see B. L. Hijmans, Jr., "Drama in Seneca's Stoicism," *Transactions of the American Philological Association,* XCVII (1966), 237–51, and A. Traina, "Lo stile 'Drammatico' del Filosofo Seneca," *Belfagor,* XIX (1964), 625–43.

12. Seneca was author of a number of consolations urging the control of one's grief, and yet reports his own excessive mourning at the death of his friend Serenus (*Ep.* 63.14); obviously Seneca means us to recognize him as the *proficiens* (not the *sapiens*) in these allusions.

13. Such allusions to himself induce several biographers to conclude that Seneca is talking about himself *at the moment;* they therefore date the *De Providentia* as being composed in 41 at the very outset of his exile. See René Waltz, *Vie de Sénèque* (Paris, 1909), pp. 101–2, and Italo Lana, *Lucio Anneo Seneca* (Turin, 1955), p. 135. There is no reason to date the *De Providentia* so early, or to assume that Seneca's work is merely autobiographical in its entirety.

14. *De Prov.* 3.2; 5.3; 5.9; 6.1.

15. For a detailed treatment of suicide and death in Seneca, see the section *"Meditatio Mortis"* of Chapter 3, pp. 68–77.

16. See, for instance, René Waltz, *Vie de Sénèque,* pp. 416–18; E. Albertini, *La Composition dans les ouvrages philosophiques de Sénèque* (Paris, 1923), pp. 44–50, 105–46; W. C. Summers, ed., *Select Letters of Seneca,* esp. pp. 222–23.

17. The Epicurean *Meditare mortem* (*Ep.* 26.8, 10) is a familiar topic in Seneca's writing; see esp. *Ep.* 54.

18. Italo Lana, *Lucio Anneo Seneca,* esp. pp. 38–39, argues that, at the time of the epistles' composition, Seneca had already achieved the "perfected" state of the *sapiens*. Seneca, we suspect, would have been startled by such a proposition, since he repeatedly insisted that wisdom was a goal to be striven for, though hardly ever to be obtained. The true *sapiens,* Seneca claimed, was as rare as the phoenix, one appearing every five hundred years (*Ep.* 42.1); for similar passages stating the rarity of wisdom, consult *De Cons. Sap.* 7.1; *De Ira* 2.10.6; *De Tranq. An.* 7.4.

19. Obviously, when that seventeenth-century polymath, Robert Burton, in his introduction ("Democritus Junior to the Reader") wishes

to demonstrate that all men are mad, sick, foolish, he recites this Senecan passage with relish (*The Anatomy of Melancholy* [1621; rpt. London, 1887], p. 42).

20. Robert C. Elliott, *The Power of Satire: Magic, Ritual, Art* (Princeton, 1960), p. 222.

21. *Aeneid* 6.3 and 3.277.

22. *Od.* 1.5.13–16. For Horace's intense fear for Vergil's life when he had been about to sail over the ocean to Greece, and Horace's invectivelike denunciation of the sea, *vid. Od.* 1.3. Concerning the general attitude in classical antiquity that dreaded and castigated the seas and sea voyages, consult W. H. Auden, *The Enchafèd Flood* (New York, 1967), esp. pp. 2–11.

23. *Cf.* Seneca's employment of *concutio, discutio,* and *iactatio* in *Ep.* 55.2. A recurrent theme in Seneca's thought explores human agitation, and vacillation: "what is it," Seneca says, "that wrestles with our soul, and prevents lasting decisions? We fluctuate from plan to plan . . ." (*Ep.* 52.1). Thus, many a man must be "shaken" from his torpor and vice, and "coerced" and "driven" (*cogo, conpello*) to goodness (*Ep.* 52.4). For philosophy alone can achieve for one a settled state of mind: "a substantial happiness which no storm can shatter" (*Ep.* 115.18).

24. Edwin Honig, *Dark Conceit: The Making of Allegory* (New York, 1966), pp. 76–77.

25. *Aeneid* 6.83–84.

26. Seneca is well aware, and reminds us, that we are all like Ulysses (*Ep.* 88.7); but he goes on to urge that Ulysses is important, not for his similarity to all men, but for his *difference:* Ulysses serves as exemplar (*Ep.* 88.7). It is precisely figures such as Hercules and Odysseus who are to be studied as exemplary (*Ep.* 52.7), and we might select from antiquity a Guide or Helper-figure (*adiutor*), and learn from him. The traditional figures from the past that Seneca himself selects are heroes who have triumphed over adversity—Socrates, Mucius, Regulus, Rutilius, Cato (*Ep.* 98.12; *cf. De Prov.* 3.4).

27. This is a traditional paradox. Speaking of his descent to the nether world, Job had conceived of a land of shadow, "where the light is as darkness" (*Job* 10:22). Milton gave the paradox renown by his description of hell: "A Dungeon horrible, on all sides round/As one great Furnace, flam'd, yet from those flames/No light, but rather darkness visible . . ." (*Paradise Lost* 1.61–63).

28. This is not Seneca's usual view; the *sapiens,* he more commonly argues, is self-sufficient; *Ep.* 9.1, 3–5, 8, 12–19; 55.4; 72.7; *De Vita Beata* 26.4; *Ad Helv.* 5.1; 13.4 *De Benef.* 7.2.4–5; 7.3.2–3; 7.8.1. Moreover, although Seneca concedes that the *sapiens* might experience the "shadows" of emotions, he most frequently emphasizes the *sapiens'*

freedom from emotions entirely: *Ep.* 85.2–16, 24–29, 41; *De Ira* 1.14.1; 2.6.3; 2.10.6–7; *De Clem.* 2.5.4–5; 2.6.1–2.

29. Concerning this doctrine, see R. D. Hicks, *Stoic and Epicurean* (London, 1910), p. 61; and E. Vernon Arnold, *Roman Stoicism* (Cambridge, 1911), p. 264.

30. *Sénèque et les religions orientales* (Bruxelles, 1967), pp. 55–56.

31. For the nearly universal conception of the "pit, hole, spring, or cavern" as gateway or entrance to the lower world, see Stith Thompson, *Motif-Index of Folk-Literature* (Bloomington, Indiana, 1966), esp. items F80 and F92. In the medieval period, Celts and other tribes similarly identified the underworld as *inside* a grave mound or *under* a hill; consult Howard Rollin Patch, "Some Elements in Mediaeval Descriptions of the Otherworld," *Publications of the Modern Language Association* XXXIII (1918), esp. 611–14.

32. See, for instance, Theodor H. Gaster, *The Oldest Stories in the World* (New York, 1952), pp. 34–42. "The standard path of the mythological adventure of the hero is a magnification of the formula represented in the rites of passage: *separation—initiation—return . . .*" asserts Joseph Campbell in *The Hero with a Thousand Faces* (New York, 1956), p. 30. Campbell sketches the outlines of a pervasive pattern enacted by innumerable gods and heroes, that he terms the "monomyth" (pp. 245–46); phases of this pattern include, among others, "The Call to Adventure," "The Crossing of the First Threshold," "The Belly of the Whale," "The Road of Trials," "Atonement with the Father," and "Apotheosis" (p. 36). A useful and thorough examination of patterns of initiation and descent is Mircea Eliade's *Rites and Symbols of Initiation: The Mysteries of Birth and Rebirth,* trans. W. R. Trask (New York, 1965).

33. "Calypso and Elysium," *Classical Journal,* LIV (1958), 2–11.

34. *Ab Urbe Condita Libri* 1.21.3.

35. *Republic* 7.514A–517B.

36. "'The Shadowy Cave': Some Speculations on a Twickenham Grotto," in *Restoration and 18th-Century Literature: Essays in Honor of Alan Dugald McKillop,* ed. Caroll Camden (Chicago, 1963), p. 77.

37. For conceptions of the sun's journey to the nether world in Egypt, see W. Max Müller, *The Mythology of All Races* (Boston, 1918), XII, 26–27; in Armenia, Mardiros H. Ananikian, *ibid.* (Boston, 1925), VII, 49–50; in Canaan, Theodor H. Gaster, *Thespis: Ritual, Myth, and Drama in the Ancient Near East* (New York, 1961), pp. 127, 215, and esp. 226–30.

38. *The Epic of Gilgamesh,* trans. N. K. Sandars (Baltimore, 1964), pp. 96–97. For Carl Jung's treatment of the underground journey as one of psychic progress, see his *Contributions to Analytical Psychology,* trans. H. G. & Mary F. Baynes (New York, 1928), 40.

39. Plutarch (?), "On the Soul," *Plutarch's Moralia,* Vol. 15, trans. F. H. Sandbach (Loeb series; Cambridge, Mass., 1969), pp. 317, 319. I am especially indebted here to the discussion by W. R. Halliday, "The Mystery Religions," *The Pagan Background of Early Christianity* (Liverpool, 1925), pp. 234–80, and by Maud Bodkin, "The Archetype of Paradise-Hades, or of Heaven and Hell," *Archetypal Patterns in Poetry* (London, 1963), pp. 90–152.

40. Concerning darkness and mud, and their role in punishing victims in Hades, as well as their employment in Orphic initiation, see Erwin Rohde, *Psyche: The Cult of Souls and Belief in Immortality Among the Greeks,* trans. W. B. Hillis ([1894]; rpt. New York, 1966), I, 240 and 248–49, n. 15.

41. For a full account of the procedure for visiting the oracle in the cave of Trophonius at Lebadeia, consult Pausanias, *Description of Greece* 9.39.1–9.40.4.

Chapter Seven

1. *Inst. Orat.* 10.1.126.

2. J. Wight Duff, *A Literary History of Rome in the Silver Age from Tiberius to Hadrian* (London, 1927), p. 230.

3. Consult Pierre Villey, *Les sources et l'évolution des essais de Montaigne,* 2 vols. (Paris, 1908), I, 15, 25, 99, esp. 214–18; Camilla H. Hay, *Montaigne, lecteur et imitateur de Sénèque* (Potiers, 1938), esp. pp. 167 ff. Bacon's *Essays* are clearly indebted to Montaigne and to Seneca; in his original dedication of the essays to the Prince of Wales, Bacon acknowledges his debt to Seneca; consult *The Works of Francis Bacon,* ed. Basil Montagu (London, 1825), I, x. On Seneca's general influence in the development of the essay, see Elbert N. S. Thompson, *The Seventeenth-Century English Essay* (Iowa City, 1926), esp. pp. 11, 42. Joseph Addison, while seemingly more Ciceronian in style and rather aloof in teasing Seneca for his *apatheia* (*Spec.* 172), nonetheless clearly perceives his debt; the *Spectator* papers are filled with quotations from Seneca's philosophical writings and references to the man; *Spec.* 476 candidly admits that Mr. Spectator has utilized two methods of composition, one employing the regularity of Cicero and Aristotle (in the critical papers), the other (in the Club papers) employing the "Wilderness of those Compositions which go by the Name of *Essays,*" the method of Seneca and Montaigne. Addison's relaxed and easy wit should remind us that his debt to Seneca is considerable. Consult the excellent new edition of *The Spectator,* ed. Donald F. Bond, 5 vols. (Oxford, 1965), and its thorough index. Charles Augustin Sainte-Beuve's *Causeries du Lundi,* or "Monday Chats," patently reveal a debt to Senecan tone and informality. Indeed, masters of the essay

have ever pursued the informal path, as the names of Dryden, Lamb, Arnold, and E. B. White make clear.

4. Ivar Lissner, *The Caesars: Might and Madness,* trans. J. M. Brownjohn (New York, 1965), p. 133.

5. M. Cornelius Fronto, *Epistula ad Verum Imp.* 2.1.6.

6. M. P. Charlesworth, *The Roman Empire* (Oxford, 1968), p. 72.

7. Catullus, *Carm.* 11.22–24.

8. Consult Michel Spanneut, *Le Stoïcisme des pères de l'église de Clément de Rome à Clément d'Alexandre* (Paris, 1957); Sister Rita Marie Bushman, "Right Reason in Stoicism and in the Christian Moral Tradition up to Saint Thomas " (unpub. Ph.D. diss., St. Louis Univ., 1947); S. Jannaccone, "S. Girolame e Seneca," *Giornale Italiano di Filologia,* XVI (1963), 326–38; and J. N. Sevenster, *Paul and Seneca* (Leiden, 1961). A convenient survey of this material is E. Vernon Arnold's "The Stoic Strain in Christianity," *Roman Stoicism* (Cambridge, 1911), pp. 408–36.

9. W. Trillitzsch, "Hieronymus und Seneca," *Mittellateinisches Jahrbuch,* II (1965), 42–54.

10. Consult P. Courcelle, "La vision cosmique de Saint Benoit," *Revue des Études Augustiniennes,* XIII (1967), 97–117; J. E. Sandys, *A History of Classical Scholarship,* 3rd ed. (Cambridge, 1921), esp. I, 653; E. Rivera de Ventosa, "Significación ideológica de las citas de Séneca en San Buenaventura," *Helmantica,* XVI (1965), 385–98; and K. D. Nothdurft, *Studien zum Einfluss Senecas auf die Philosophie und Theologie des zwölften Jahrhunderts* (Leiden, 1963).

11. Roger Bacon, *The "Opus Majus" of Roger Bacon,* ed. J. H. Bridges, 2 vols. (Oxford, 1897), esp. I, 290–91.

12. E. G. Bourne, "Seneca and the Discovery of America," *Essays in Historical Criticism* (New York, 1901), pp. 219–24.

13. *Sir Thomas Pope Blount's Essays on Several Subjects,* 3rd ed. (London, 1697), Essay IV, p. 138.

14. Petrarch's *Epistles* are modeled upon Seneca's; see Edward H. R. Tatham, *Francesco Petrarca: The First Modern Man of Letters* (London, 1925), I, 429; W. Trillitzsch, "Erasmus und Seneca," *Philologus,* CIX (1965), 270–93; J. Espiner-Scott, " Sénèque dans la prose anglaise de More à Lyly (1500–1580)," *Revue de Littérature Comparée,* XXXIV (1960), 177–95; A. Rothe, *Quevedo und Seneca: Untersuchungen zu den Frühschriften Quevedos* (Geneva, 1965); and Léontine Zanta, *La Renaissance du Stoïcisme au XVIᵉ siècle* (Paris, 1914), treating particularly the works of Justus Lipsius and Guillaume Du Vair.

15. W. Lee Ustick, "Changing Ideals of Aristocratic Character and Conduct in Seventeenth-Century England," *Modern Philology,* XXX (1932), 147–66.

16. George Williamson, *The Senecan Amble: A Study in Prose Form from Bacon to Collier* (Chicago, 1951).

17. See esp. John W. Cunliffe, *The Influence of Seneca on Elizabethan Tragedy* (London, 1893).

18. The very nature of their material reveals a debt to Euripedes and Seneca: Corneille's *Medée* (1634), *Le Morte de Pompée* (1643), *Oedipe* (1659), and Racine's *Iphigénie* (1674), *Phèdre* (1677), and esp. the *Andromache* (1667). On Racine and Seneca, see also E. Paratore, "De Gentilitatis Sumptuaria Ratione apud Senecam," *Latinitas,* XIII (1965), 166–71. On the increasing Stoical quality of Dryden's heroical plays, see John A. Winterbottom, "Stoicism in Dryden's Tragedies," *Journal of English and Germanic Philology,* LXI (1962), 868–83.

19. André Bridoux, *Le Stoicisme et son influence* (Paris, 1966), pp. 224–26.

20. Ester A. Tiffany, "Shaftesbury as Stoic," *Publications of The Modern Language Association,* XXXVIII (1923), 642–84.

21. Henry W. Sams, "Anti-Stoicism in Seventeenth- and Early Eighteenth-Century England," *Studies in Philology,* XLI (1944), 65–78; see also Rudolf Kirk's introduction to Justus Lipsius, *Two Bookes of Constancie* (New Brunswick, N.J., 1939), pp. 39–46 for Lipsius' reservations about Stoicism; these objections are often repeated in the next two centuries.

22. Robert Voitle, "Stoicism and Samuel Johnson" (*Studies in Philology,* Extra Series No. 4, January, 1967), *Essays in English Literature of the Classical Period Presented to Dougald MacMillan,* ed. Daniel W. Patterson and Albrecht B. Strauss, p. 108.

23. Rousseau's description of Nature and Providence is distinctly Senecan; consult Charles W. Hendel, *Jean-Jaques Rousseau: Moralist,* 2 vols. (London, 1934), I, 232 ff., and also Chap. I, "Avec Socrate et le Divin Platon, Je m'exerce à marcher sur les pas de Caton," I, 1–19. See also P. Bosshard, "Die Beziehungen zwischen Rousseaus zweiten Discours und dem 90 Brief von Seneca" (unpub. diss., Zurich, 1967).

24. An almost verbatim rendering of *Ep.* 121.10: *Jam non consilio bonus, sed more eo perductus, ut non tantum recte facere possim, sed nisi recte facere non possim* ("No longer good deliberately, but induced by habit to such a point that I not only can act rightly but can do nothing else").

25. Emerson's *Journals* (esp. Vols. I–VI, 1819–38) are filled with references to Seneca (and Montaigne). At times, Emerson sounds just the note of Senecan zeal for collecting grand thoughts, as when he instructs himself to compile the sayings of great men: "Make your own Bible. Select & Collect all those words and sentences that in all your reading have been to you like the blast of trumpet out of Shak-

spear, Seneca, Moses, John, & Paul," *The Journals and Miscellaneous Notebooks of Ralph Waldo Emerson,* ed. William H. Gilman *et al.,* 8 Vols (Cambridge, Mass., 1960–70), V, 186; cf. V, 466.

26. Thomas Babington Macaulay, "Lord Bacon," *Critical and Historical Essays* (New York, 1875), pp. 389 ff.

27. Consult esp. Calvin O. Schrag, Ch. 4: "Death and Transitoriness," *Existence and Freedom: Towards an Ontology of Human Finitude* (Evanston, Ill., 1961), pp. 95–118.

28. Monsieur A. Fronton, in his "Camus entre le Paganisme et le Christianisme," *La table ronde,* Feb. 1960, pp. 114–19, places considerable emphasis upon a Stoic reading of Camus. See also Henri Peyre, "Camus the Pagan," *Yale French Studies,* XXV (1960), 20–25.

29. Paul Tillich, *The Courage to Be* (New Haven, 1952), treats specifically of the Stoics, pp. 9–17. The quotation in the text is from p. 9.

30. The Institute "Luis Vives" de Filosofía celebrated the centennial, April 19–23, 1965, in Madrid; their collection of essays is entitled *Estudios Sobre Séneca: Ponencias y Comunicaciones* (Madrid, 1966); the Congreso Internacional de Filosofía met at Cordova, Sept. 7–12, 1965, and their *Actas del Congreso Internacional de Filosofía* were published in 3 Vols. (Cordova, 1965; Madrid, 1966, 1967).

31. *Divina Commedia:* "Inferno," 4.141.

32. *Canterbury Tales:* "The Monk's Tale," 6.2495–98.

Selected Bibliography

•

PRIMARY SOURCES

1. Latin Texts

HAASE, F., ed. *L. Annaei Senecae Opera Quae Supersunt.* 3 vols. Leipzig: Teubner, 1852. Fine edition of Seneca.

HERMES, E., HOSIUS, C., GERCKE, A., & HENSE, O., eds. *L. Annaei Senecae opera quae supersunt.* . . . 3 vols. Leipzig: Teubner, 1898–1907. The standard text.

PEIPER, R. & RICHTER, G., eds. *L. Annaei Senecae Tragoediae.* Leipzig: Teubner, 1902. A standard, and often preferred, edition of the plays.

REYNOLDS, L. D., ed. *Annaei Senecae Ad Lucilium Epistulae Morales.* 2 vols. Oxford: Clarendon Press, 1965. The best edition of the *Letters* yet to appear.

SUMMERS, W. C., ed. *Select Letters of Seneca.* London: Macmillan, 1910. Good introduction on style and syntax in the only edition in English with explanatory notes.

2. English Translations

BARKER, E. P. *Seneca's Letters to Lucilius.* 2 vols. Oxford: Clarendon Press, 1932. Adequate translation, but fails to capture Seneca's animated style.

CAMPBELL, R. *Seneca, Letters from a Stoic: Epistulae Morales ad Lucilium.* Selected and translated with an Introduction. Baltimore: Penguin Books, 1969. Lively translation of selected letters, in clear prose.

Loeb Series:

BASORE, J. W., ed. *Seneca, Moral Essays.* 3 vols. New York: G. P. Putnam's Sons; Cambridge, Mass.: Harvard University Press; & London: William Heinemann, 1928–35.

CORCORAN, T. H., ed. *Seneca, Natural Questions.* 2 vols. Cambridge, Mass.: Harvard University Press; London: William Heinemann, 1971.

165

GUMMERE, R. M., ed. *Seneca, ad Lucilium Epistulae Morales.* 3 vols. New York: G. P. Putnam's Sons; London: William Heinemann, 1917–25.

The Loeb is the only series in English containing a translation (and Latin text) of all of Seneca's extant prose works. On the whole, the translations are clear and readable as well as quite literal.

3. Bibliographies

COFFEY, M. "Seneca, Apocolocyntosis 1922–1958," *Lustrum,* VI (1961), 239–271.

———. "Senecan Tragedies including pseudo-Senecan *Octavia* and Epigrams attributed to Seneca. Report for the years 1922–1955," *Lustrum,* II (1957), 113–86. Coffey's surveys are incisive and thorough, with extensive analysis of major works.

MOTTO, A. L. "Recent Scholarship on Seneca's Prose Works, 1940–1957," *Classical World,* LIV (1960), 13–18, 37–48, 70–71; "Addenda, 1957–1958" (1961), 111–12.

———. "Seneca's Prose Writings: A Decade of Scholarship, 1958–1968," *Classical World,* LXIV (1971), 141–58, 177–86, 191. These two surveys of scholarship offer brief commentary on individual items and extensive critical evaluation of major works.

SECONDARY SOURCES

ABEL, K. *Bauformen in Senecas Dialogen. Fünf Strukturanalysen: dial. 6, 11, 12, 1 und 2.* Heidelberg: Carl Winter, 1967. Analyzes the rhetorical form of the *Ad Marc., Ad Helv., Ad Polyb., De Prov.,* and *De Cons. Sap.,* clearly demonstrating a dialogue's structure, from simple beginnings, through mounting debates, to forceful climax.

ARNOLD, E. V. *Roman Stoicism.* Cambridge: Cambridge University Press, 1911. The most thorough and systematic presentation in English of Roman Stoicism.

BOURGERY, A. *Sénèque Prosateur.* Paris: Société D'Édition "Les Belles Lettres," 1922. A lengthy account of Senecan style, syntax, grammar, and vocabulary.

BRINCKMANN, W. *Der Begriff der Freundschaft in Senecas Briefen.* Cologne: Gouder and Hansen, 1963. Traces past traditions and *topoi* concerning friendship and examines the nature of this significant concept in Seneca's *Letters.*

CUNLIFFE, J. W. *The Influence of Seneca on Elizabethan Tragedy.* London: Macmillan, 1893. Ground-breaking analysis of Seneca's influence upon the Elizabethans.

GRIMAL, P. *Sénèque, sa vie, son oeuvre, sa philosophie.* Paris: Presses Universitaires de France, 1948. A brief, well-written account of Seneca's life and philosophy with extracts from his prose in French translation.

GUMMERE, R. M. *Seneca the Philosopher and his Modern Message.* Boston: Marshall Jones, 1922. A small, nontechnical volume surveying the extensive influence in all ages of Senecan humanism, thought, and style.

HERRMANN, L. *Le Théâtre de Sénèque.* Paris: Société D'Édition "Les Belles Lettres," 1924. Discussion of general problems relating to Senecan drama; Herrmann is best in treating characters, ideas, *topoi.*

HOLLAND, F. *Seneca.* London: Longmans, Green, 1920. The only published biography in English, this book, scantily annotated, gives a standard chronological account of Seneca's life and contains a brief chapter on his philosophy.

LANA, I. *Lucio Anneo Seneca.* Turin: Loescher, 1955. A well-annotated book stressing the philosopher's difficult role as moralist *and* politician; Seneca's works are treated chiefly from a biographical point of view.

MARCHESI, C. *Seneca.* Milan: Guiseppe Principato, 1934. Next to Waltz's book, this is the most thorough biography. With full scholarly apparatus, it describes Seneca's life, writings, and philosophy.

MENDELL, C. W. *Our Seneca.* New Haven: Yale University Press, 1941. One of the few books in English devoted to Seneca as dramatist. Unfortunately, Mendell's book is digressive and without annotation and is preoccupied with detailed comparisons of Senecan and Greek drama.

MOTTO, A. L. *Seneca Sourcebook: Guide to the Thought of Lucius Annaeus Seneca.* Amsterdam: A. M. Hakkert, 1970. An alphabetical citation of the fundamental ideas and their recurrence in the extant prose works.

POHLENZ, M. *Die Stoa, Geschichte einer geistigen Bewegung.* 2 vols. Göttingen: Vandenhoeck and Ruprecht, 1948–49. The most thorough history of the Old, Middle, and New Stoa, with invaluable notes and a brief survey of the Stoa in the Middle Ages and the modern world.

REGENBOGEN, O. *Schmerz und Tod in den Tragödien Senecas.* 2d ed. Darmstadt: Wissenschaftliche Buchgesellschaft, 1963. A small but important study which early (1927) analyzed in detail psychological scenes of pain and suffering in the plays. The author believes that Senecan analyses of frenzy and anguish are based upon Stoic principles.

WALTZ, R. *Vie de Sénèque*. Paris: Librairie Académique, 1909. This major biography, scholarly and well documented, emphasizes Seneca's important role in politics and presents a vivid picture of the philosopher's milieu.

ZELLER, E. *Stoics, Epicureans and Sceptics*, trans. O. J. Reichel. Rev. ed. London: Longmans, Green, 1879. The standard study of the origins and development of the major Hellenistic philosophies; brilliantly annotated.

Index